Negotiating *MANAGED CARE CONTRACTS*

Disclaimer

Negotiating MANAGED CARE CONTRACTS

The Medical Management Institute

McGraw-Hill, Inc.
New York St. Louis San Francisco Auckland Bogatá Caracas
Lisbon London Madrid Mexico Milan Montreal New Delhi Paris
San Juan Singapore Sydney Tokyo Toronto

A Product of McGraw-Hill, Inc.

NEGOTIATING MANAGED CARE CONTRACTS

2 3 4 5 6 7 8 9 0 MAL MAL954

ISBN 0-07-600705-7

This book was composed and set in Goudy
by Huron Valley Graphics, Inc.

Table of Contents

About the Authors

The co-authors, Robert D. Keene and Fred F. Naus, founded The Medical Management Institute in response to the medical community's need for continuing education in areas other than medicine. In the 1990s, with the public's demand for healthcare reform, the requirement for keeping current in issues such as managed care, Medicare, and procedural coding have become more pressing than ever. This publication is one of many they have created in direct response to the medical community's informational needs.

Robert D. Keene, Chairman-CEO of The Medical Management Institute, is a consultant with particular expertise in financial planning and operational budgets, personnel management, and fiscal intermediaries including Medicare, managed care organizations and other payors.

Fred F. Naus, President of The Medical Management Institute, is a medical practice management consultant and computer systems analyst with over 20 years' experience in problem solving, dealing with third party payors, computer system selection, and cost-effective management techniques for computerized practices.

PREFACE

As interest in healthcare reform continues to grow, managed care is a reality that must be faced. Based on the perception by many that a crisis in financing healthcare exists, the call has gone out for widespread changes. In the past, while groups such as the elderly and disabled have "chalked up" several medical coverage improvements, even these sectors have experienced increasing difficulty in gaining access to needed care because of increased attention to the bottom line.

Over the past decade, many physicians have participated in one or several managed care plans. By not always fully understanding the ramifications of these arrangements, some found themselves in unexpected situations. For example, a physician may have been forced to lower costs due to increased competition. Others may now be facing financial setbacks because they did not forecast the financial impact of their arrangements. Where in the past physicians might have wished to keep their hands off the business end of their practices, examples such as these demonstrate this is no longer feasible. In light of President Clinton's proposed Health Security Act, a practice's ability to negotiate a fair but profitable managed care contract will be key to survival.

Negotiating Managed Care Contracts provides the information physicians need to wind their way through the managed care maze. Managed care is discussed in the context of the long history of healthcare reform, with a review of the reform proposals up for consideration on Capitol Hill. The different types of managed care plans are covered along with rules and regulations governing them. This book provides guidance for a practice to determine whether it is ready to participate in managed care, to evaluate contracts, and to implement managed care processes. Properly negotiating managed care contracts can help physicians attract new patients and increase net income while minimizing their economic liabilities.

The authors with to thank their team of technical/management consultants and administrative staff for their assistance, planning, and hard work.

CHAPTER I

Introduction

Background

During the eighty years between this nation's twenty-sixth and forty-fourth Presidents countless leaders, private citizens, commissions, and task forces have recommended ways to finance healthcare. All these groups and Presidents have warned about the dangers of an impending crisis in this area, and many have called for widespread changes in the American medical system. Healthcare thus has been one of the most significant controversies in the American political debate during the last hundred years, but despite this century of contention, most attempts to enact comprehensive healthcare reform in the United States have failed.

Many people believe that these proposed reforms have failed because of the definition of *national health insurance*, a term that has been consistently redefined in the United States. The lack of agreement on the meaning of this concept can explain why the United States has failed to enact comprehensive health coverage. Today a consensus is growing that the American healthcare sector is nearing a crisis of unprecedented proportions and that we must act now to prevent chaos. Yet no one seems to know what we should do, what features of a health plan are essential, or even what type of universal coverage and cost containment should be established.

A History of Medical Reform

In 1912 Theodore Roosevelt, running for President against Woodrow Wilson, endorsed the Progressive party platform, which pledged "protection against the hazard of sickness." This plan included the institution of a system of social insurance for use by all Americans. However, Wilson won the election, and medical reform disappeared from the Federal agenda for almost a decade. Later, when other progressive reformers introduced legislation to establish a state-run insurance system, the state medical societies, the National Medical Society, the American Federation of Labor, and most businesses opposed it. However, the most devastating blow to significant health insurance reform occurred in the early 1920s, when the charge was made that such coverage was "un-American." It was argued that social health coverage had been invented in Germany and thus was a foreign import. This argument proved to be so effective that labeling health insurance "alien" ever since has had appeal to critics of national health insurance.

The first positive step toward insuring Americans for medical care occurred in 1930, during the great depression, when great numbers of Americans turned to Franklin D. Roosevelt to solve many of the nation's problems. At that time politicians in Washington responded. Many of the protections we now take for granted—Social Security, unemployment insurance, the Federal Deposit Insurance Corporation, fair labor laws—were born during FDR's administration. At that time, Americans were inclined to have faith in the government. Most believed that Washington could make a positive difference, and often it was able to do so.

When the Social Security Act finally reached Congress, however, the portion of the Senate's Social Security bill calling for further study of public health insurance had been stricken unanimously by the Ways and Means Committee. The administration was convinced that any mention of national healthcare would cause the Social Security Act to be defeated. When Roosevelt submitted his proposal to Congress, there was nothing in the plan dealing with healthcare coverage.

Even though Roosevelt was very popular, too much power was held by organized medicine and the opposition political party to permit the enactment of healthcare reform. Given the absence of public involvement in and understanding of the problem, no effective citizens' organizations surfaced to counter the objections of the opposing lobbyists during the 1930s and 1940s.

Although Roosevelt continually pledged to support national health insurance, World War II absorbed most of his attention. The battle over health insurance paled in comparison to the real-life battles raging overseas.

However, by the late 1940s the benefits of modern medicine had become unavailable to Americans whose employers did not provide comprehensive health insurance as a fringe benefit for their workers and to those who could not afford to purchase private coverage. President Harry

Truman decided that it was time to address the situation by renewing the fight for universal health insurance. In September 1945 he sent a message to Congress outlining a proposed economic bill of rights for every American citizen. At that time he spoke of the right to adequate medical care, the opportunity to achieve and enjoy good health, and the right to adequate protection from the economic fears that accompany sickness. Under his plan people would continue to receive healthcare as before, with one difference: Receipt of services from the medical profession would not depend on how much one could afford to pay.

Organized medicine mounted an expensive and effective campaign against Truman. It was able to invoke the fear of communism by claiming that supporters of reform, including the President, believed in a "socialistic state". The President fought back by stating that Americans were the most insurance-minded people in the world. Truman believed that the public would not be deterred from pursuing universal health insurance just because some people mislabeled it socialized medicine, but he was wrong. Truman left office in 1953, having fought and lost one of the most bruising battles in history on behalf of comprehensive healthcare reform.

The defeat of Truman's proposal led his supporters to change their strategy. Instead of trying to sell the concept of insuring everyone, the emphasis was shifted to protecting only the aged. This made sense, because the elderly were generally in greater need of medical services. Since Social Security beneficiaries were older, they had greater medical needs; since they were retired, they lacked the benefits of group enrollment through employment. As their health insurance costs rose, most of the elderly lost their private coverage. Government was once again called on to respond, and this time it did. Soon after the 1964 election Medicare and Medicaid legislation was enacted and then implemented, after what President Lyndon Johnson described as the largest effort involving resource management this nation has ever undertaken. There were successes and failures in the administration of the program during the ensuing thirty years, but most of the elderly gained access to medical care.

In 1971, President Richard Nixon held extensive hearings on healthcare insurance and hearings also were conducted by the House Ways and Means Committee. In 1972 Medicare was extended to cover the disabled. In 1974 administrative support of comprehensive health insurance seemed to ensure that healthcare financial mechanisms would be restructured. However, by July 1974 over twenty-two different healthcare reform bills were introduced to the Congress, a situation similar to that of the early 1990s.

Even with all these options to consider, many legislators were optimistic that sweeping legislation would soon assure medical coverage for all American citizens. However, because of the number of options presented, no action could be agreed on, and Watergate became the prime focus of the remainder of Nixon's term. Furthermore, a conflict had arisen among the individuals involved with one group endorsing comprehensive change (saying we need it now) and another favoring an incremental approach (saying we must proceed slowly, one step at a time). President Ronald Reagan made it clear that he wanted competition rather than government intervention. Therefore, the United States saw the growth of managed care, diagnosis-related groups (DRGs), and other administrative changes to the medical reimbursement system, with no program for providing services to individuals who lacked medical insurance coverage.

Has the Time Finally Arrived?

Many people believe that the American healthcare system has become more complicated, and the dissatisfaction of large portions of the electorate with Washington has intensified. Most experts agree that the United States is close to or is already experiencing a healthcare catastrophe. Many analysts are now predicting that the various interested parties—providers, payers, and patients—will have no choice but to negotiate and make compromises about their differences. The renewed sense of optimism and resolve rests primarily on two factors: (1) The country is better able to apply lessons learned from past health reform failures as well as from successes with the Medicare program, and (2) former adversaries are eager to cooperate, including businesses (which traditionally oppose any form of government intervention) and labor (which traditionally negotiates for higher wages and benefits regardless of the economic climate). Both sides have selected a common enemy - healthcare costs—and have united to fight against it.

During the 1990s, as occurred during the 1960s with Medicare, the need for change has surfaced from many sources simultaneously:

- Employers, ravaged by increasing healthcare premiums and unwilling to cut wages, want to decrease the cost of employee healthcare to free funds for research and development.
- The government wants to reduce the deficit by containing inflationary increases in Medicare and Medicaid costs, freeing funds for other domestic concerns.
- Many doctors and hospitals want to replace intrusion into their clinical decisions with more effective ways to control costs.

Has the time finally arrived? What's new is that many insured and uninsured are unhappy and our government and industry officials believe the healthcare system is coming apart. Many people contend that the 1990s is the time to act and that we are closer than ever to acting. What, if any, actions are likely to be taken? Will managed care plans of some kind be adopted? We believe that a lot of new managed care concepts will be introduced, and traditional managed care services will continue to expand.

The Managed Competition Proposals

The numerous proposals for healthcare reform currently before Congress all have one thing in common: They tout managed competition in one way or another. Also, the various bills mirror many of the recommendations of the Jackson Hole group. This group of top health policymakers who meet frequently in the Wyoming mountains supports major revisions to health insurance, including the implementation of managed competition, which the Clinton administration adopted as its starting point for initiating reform.

Among the Jackson Hole plan's visionary goals are insuring everyone, controlling costs and improving the quality of medical care. (Other health policy analysts contended that while any two of these goals can be achieved through reform, a combination of any two will make a third a financial and political impossibility.) These goals, the Jackson Hole group maintains, can be realized by pressuring providers (hospitals, doctors, home healthcare agencies, etc.) and insurers to organize themselves into comprehensive delivery systems and compete for insureds through uniform measures of cost and clinical effectiveness (outcomes data and patient satisfaction data may be used for this purpose). The complete delivery systems would be required to offer comprehensive, standardized benefits, in part so that potential insureds will be able to compare prices.

Other Healthcare Reform Plans Seriously Being Considered

Sponsor	*Chafee*	*Cooper/Breaux*	*Gramm*	*McDermott*	*Michel*
Coverage	Employers must offer, but do not have to pay for insurance; everyone must buy it. Universal by 2000.	Individuals pay for insurance but are not required to buy it. (Also known as "Clinton Lite").	Employers must offer, but do not have to pay for insurance. Individuals not required to buy it.	Universal coverage for all Americans.	Employers must offer, but do not have to pay for insurance. Individuals not required to buy it.
Benefits	Choose between: standard benefits (doctor, hospital, drug, prevention) or catastrophic coverage. Details to be developed.	Not yet specified. National health board to recommend standard package to Congress for yes or no vote.	No standard package. Funds in medical IRAs buy catastrophic insurance to pay expenses over $3,000 annually.	Standard benefits (doctor, hospital, drug, prevention, mental health); details developed by national board. Includes long-term care.	Establishes medical IRAs to pay healthcare expenses. Benefits not otherwise specified.

Sponsor	*Chafee*	*Cooper/Breaux*	*Gramm*	*McDermott*	*Michel*
Financing	Individuals responsible for entire premium. Low-income subsidies.	Individuals responsible for entire premium. Low-income subsidies.	Individuals responsible for entire premium.	Government pays costs via taxes on employers, employees, tobacco.	Individuals responsible for entire premium.
Cost Controls	Through market forces. Cut Medicare, Medicaid growth. Malpractice caps. Administrative reform.	Through market forces. No caps on private sector or government programs. Malpractice caps. Administrative reform.	Through market forces. Cut Medicare, Medicaid growth. Malpractice caps. Administrative reform.	National health budget. Limits on provider rates. Administrative reform.	Through market forces. No caps on private, Medicare, Medicaid spending. Malpractice caps. Administrative reform.
Impact on Medicare	Medicare remains for now. No drug or other new benefits. Higher incomes pay more.	Medicare remains. More preventive, but no drug, coverage. Higher incomes pay more.	Medicare remains. No new benefits.	Eliminates Medicare; beneficiaries placed in national system.	Medicare remains. No drug or other new benefits. Higher incomes pay more.
Structure	Small employers may form purchasing groups to buy insurance.	Purchasing groups required, except for large firms.	Small employers may form purchasing groups to buy insurance.	Federal standards, states administer program.	Small employers may form purchasing groups to buy insurance.

Source: AARP

President Clinton's Healthcare Plan

President Clinton has adapted a version of managed competition that blends market-based and government-based reforms. It relies on market focus to make insurance companies compete on the basis of quality and cost. It uses the government to rein in the remaining costs of providing medical care to guarantee universal coverage (see Figure 1-1).

The Clinton Administration's proposal, the Health Security Act of 1993, is based upon six basic principles: Security, Simplicity, Savings, Choice, Quality, and Responsibility.

- **Security:** Each American would have universally guaranteed and comprehensive healthcare benefits that he or she would never lose.

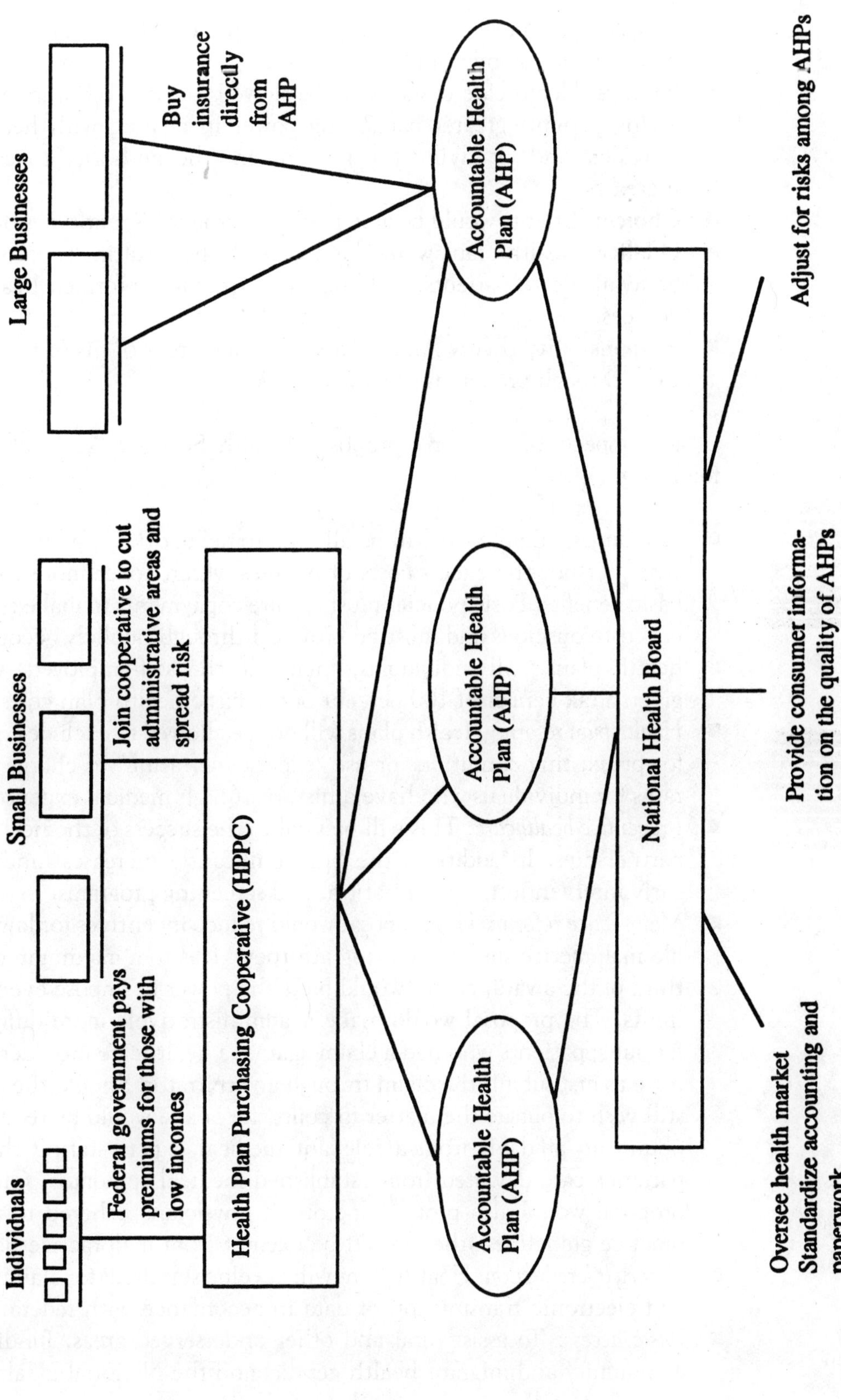

Figure 1-1 The Financing of Health Care Delivery under Managed Competition

- **Simplicity:** Bureaucracy and paper work would be reduced; there would be one standardized claims form.
- **Savings:** Healthcare costs would be slowed to the level of inflation by giving patients greater bargaining power in dealing with healthcare providers and by giving the government the authority to cap rate increases.
- **Choice:** Patients would be able to choose from different types of plans.
- **Quality:** Health plans would be reviewed; the resulting reports would be available to patients enabling them to make informed healthcare choices.
- **Responsibility:** Every American would pay a part of his or her health care, through premiums or cost sharing.

Key aspects of Clinton's proposed Health Security Act include the following:

- *Tax fairness:* Employers will be allowed to deduct the basic health plan costs but not the excess costs of policies which cover more than the basic benefits. Basic policies must require copayments to make consumers cost-conscious and must be provided through publicly accountable health plans. All individuals, including the self-employed, will be given a tax benefit of 100 percent of the basic health plan costs.
- *Health plan reform:* Health plans will not be allowed to exclude coverage for preexisting conditions or use "experience rating" to charge higher rates for individuals who have a history of high medical expenses.
- *Preventive healthcare:* This will be vital to the success of the new health partnerships. In addition, the bill significantly increases funding for early intervention, immunization, and screening programs.
- *Malpractice reform:* The proposal would reduce incentives for lawyers to file malpractice suits by limiting attorneys' fees to a maximum of one-third of the award. States would have the power to impose even lower limits. The proposal would make it administratively more difficult to file suits; patients who had a claim against a healthcare provider would have to first submit the claim through an arbitrator. Should the patient still wish to pursue the matter in court, he or she would be required to obtain an affidavit from a relevant medical expert stating that the patient's care deviated from established medical standards. Clinton's proposal would also protect doctors; if physicians adhered to federal practice guidelines, they would be exempt from malpractice liability.
- *Paperwork reduction:* Health plans will develop standards for claims forms and electronic transmission of data in accordance with federal goals.
- *Basic access:* To assist rural and other underserved areas, funding for community and migrant health centers and the National Health Service Corps will be increased substantially.
- *Cost:* Representative Cooper (D-TN) indicates that the bill would cost $30 billion per year, as opposed to an estimated $400 billion to imple-

ment the Waxman/Dingell single-payor healthcare reform proposal. To pay for the program, the Administration proposes to generate approximately $10 billion by eliminating the tax deductibility of healthcare benefits that exceed the basic benefit package. The bill also would raise $12 billion by eliminating disproportionate share payments to hospitals with an unusually high percentage of Medicaid patients. Finally, the bill would raise approximately $8 billion in revenues by eliminating the earnings limit on Medicare premiums. In the end, the President believes that the program would be budget-neutral. At the local level, premiums would be negotiated among the various alliances and health insurance companies. At the national level, a healthcare budget would be formed to control the growth of healthcare spending and cost. The main fund source would come from premiums paid to the health alliances. Additional sources would include: savings from Medicare/Medicaid, sin taxes, increased corporate tax collections and by simplifying the healthcare system's administration and paperwork.

- *State Plans:* They have been encouraged to "incubate" new ideas for healthcare delivery systems and to develop plans pertinent to their individual needs.

Potential Changes During the Clinton Presidency

It has been suggested that the following changes in the Clinton Plan may occur over the next few years.

1. A takeover by the government of healthcare (Canadian system)
2. Pay or play (employer provides insurance or pays a payroll tax)
3. Managed competition incentives by pooling individuals and companies into large purchasing groups so that they can compete with large corporations (60 to 70 percent of conservative democrats and most Republicans support this idea).

Many elected officials are still asking where the money will come from:

1. Additional taxes
2. Market control
3. Price control by the government

No other country has ever tried managed competition and no one knows how it would work. Some states most likely will continue with local reforms. Some members of Congress will push for a government-run health system or for keeping the government out of medicine. Both groups face an uphill battle.

Is the medical community staring down the barrel of 1970s-style price controls? Will rationing of medical care come to pass? How will medical delivery fare under national limits on spending? Can a national health board reach agreements that will reduce costs? How will a managed competition plan affect a particular practice and individual patients? These, as well as many other unanswered questions, plague the Clinton administration.

One approach that has been discussed is managed competition. This concept is intended to encourage providers and insurance companies to form accountable health plans (AHPs), which will compete for enrollees on the basis of cost and quality, offering insurance and healthcare as a single product. Other components would include the following:

- A national health board would be created to define a uniform set of health benefits. AHPs would have to offer those benefits to all applying enrollees.
- Employers and individuals purchasing coverage through federally qualified AHPs could receive tax advantages by purchasing the least costly benefit plans or the basic plan.
- A copayment would be required for all services except preventive care.
- AHPs in all likelihood would be state-chartered organizations, offering enrollees a menu of insurance plans. Individuals or companies would then select the desired plan.
- Administrative expenses would be funded by a surcharge on the premium per enrollee in each plan.
- All individuals except employees of very large businesses (1,000 or more employees) would join health plan purchasing cooperatives (HPPCs).
- Medicare would essentially remain as it is for now; however, individual Medicare beneficiaries could join an HPPC.
- Medicaid would be replaced by HPPCs and the unemployed without coverage would be covered by HPPCs as well.
- Local AHPs will link insurers, hospitals, clinics and doctors; they will be paid through capitation fees negotiated by each group or set by the state.

The mechanisms that may be employed to effect these changes include budgeting, malpractice reform, employer involvement and incentives, and administrative cost containment.

Global Budgeting: What It Does and Does Not Mean

How will the global concept work in conjunction with state and national budgets? There will be a group appointed by Congress (much like the Physician Payment Review Committee) that decides how much the country will spend on healthcare in any single year; when prices exceed that amount, prices will be adjusted downward. Global budgeting means price setting. Decisions about spending will be centralized and this will have an enormous impact on healthcare in the United States. Patients still will be able to see a selected physician and go to a selected hospital; however, doctors and hospitals will have capitation limits, as some have now through HMOs. This also will create a greater role for primary care physicians.

Based on discussions with persons in policy-making positions, there are a lot of misconceptions about this area. Further, it is far from certain what role, if any, global budgeting will play in a final healthcare reform package. There are important constituencies on both sides of this issue. For example, Representative Pete Stark (D-CA) is strongly in favor of having a global budget mechanism in any reform package, while Representative Jim Cooper (D-TN) has indicated his opposition to global budgets.

There are currently three broad categories of global budgeting mechanisms which might be implemented:

1. President Clinton may wish to control prices for every cost input item in the industry. However, the Clinton people have not expressed interest in pursuing this type of strategy. The difficulties that the Healthcare Financing Administration (HCFA) has experienced in setting 7,000 fees under the new medicare resource-based relative value scale (RBRVS) are widely known. Setting input prices for every aspect of the entire industry would be so difficult that it would take a long time to enact legislation that included this provision.

2. Global budgets may be used to establish spending limits for designated groups or geographic areas. For example, under managed competition, a limit might be established on the total amount of money a particular HPPC could pay to provide healthcare for the people in its service area. However, the spending limit could have the effect of establishing once and for all a "super capitated group purchasing effort" whereby all services to an insured are paid by a negotiated amount of money each month. A problem arises, of course, when the plan overshoots its spending budget. If funds are immediately cut off once the fund has deployed its resources, care must be rationed. In other proposals, however, the overage is made up in subsequent years. The Clinton people have discussed global budgets along the lines described here but have not been specific about the form enforcement would take if the budgeted target is exceeded.

3. A final use of global budgets would be one in which targets were established and then "moral suasion" was used to ensure cost containment. In other words, payers and providers would be held up to scrutiny, and their ability to obtain business in subsequent years would be based on their ability to meet budgets today. The Clinton administration may employ global budgets in this manner as well.

Malpractice Reform

Most people agree that the current system is inequitable and inefficient. Often the system leads to defensive medicine and overprovision of services.

Doctors frequently feel pressured to do more when less is sufficient; thus, it is imperative that Congress pass some type of tort reform legislation.

Employer Contributions (Pay or Play)

Employers would be able to purchase health insurance in the private market or contribute to a fund that would enable their employees to obtain health coverage. Under this plan, the law would require employers to purchase coverage; this would no longer be an option.

There would in all likelihood be public/private systems in conjunction with a public sponsor. This sponsor would help place people in private health insurance programs. The system would have to be phased in, probably over one to three years, because small businesses would be unable to adapt all at once.

Congress and the national board would mandate a "minimal" package that would have to be provided regardless of employer/employee preferences.

Administrative Costs

There are at least 1500 companies offering various forms of healthcare insurance. Each one may have multiple plans, each with its own paperwork requirements. Defensive medicine is often blamed for increasing the number of tests physicians request. The Clinton proposal includes assumptions that decreased administrative costs can pay for much of the proposed increases in coverage.

A national healthcare system has been proposed many times during the last twenty years, but big business and physicians did not agree that it was appropriate or right for the country. This time business will not attempt to fend off future government intrusion into medical reimbursement. Because of cost increases, businesses and many medical organizations have switched sides.

Medical Economics conducted a survey of practicing physicians to assess the American healthcare system. That journal asked the following questions: Is there a crisis? If so, what are the causes? What are the solutions? [1]

The findings were that doctors are dissatisfied with today's healthcare system. More than 80 percent agree that there is a crisis, 45 percent believe that fundamental changes are needed, and 99 percent think that some change is needed. More than 75 percent call for those changes to be made within the next five years. Like business, the private sector has shifted away from accepting the status quo.

Who Would Be Covered?

Everyone would have insurance either through his or her job or through quasi-public insurance pools. The pools would be administered by private

[1] *Medical Economics*, "How Doctors Would Cure America's Health Care Crisis", Sept., 1992.

insurance companies and financed by state and federal government funds, employer premiums, and individual premiums. Insurance companies would be prohibited from denying coverage because of an individual's health history. Medicaid would be absorbed into this program.

Who Would Pay?

Under Clinton's plan, patients would have to pay for their healthcare in two ways: monthly premiums and per-service cost sharing amounts. Premiums would be locally-based and would depend on the average cost of healthcare in each alliance area. Cost sharing amounts would vary with the type of health plan selected. There are special rules for the self-employed, part-time workers, the unemployed, retirees, and the indigent (Figure 1-2).

- *Self-employed.* They would pay the premium for the employer and employee, but the premium would be fully tax deductible. If a firm earned less than $24,000 per year, it would be eligible for government subsidies.
- *Part-time workers.* Normally, they would contribute up to 20 percent of their premiums, with their employer paying a pro-rata share based on the number of hours worked.
- *Unemployed individuals.* They would be required to pay the entire premium, but could receive government assistance, if they qualified.
- *Retirees.* The government would pay the employer share of retirees' premiums who were not yet eligible for Medicare.

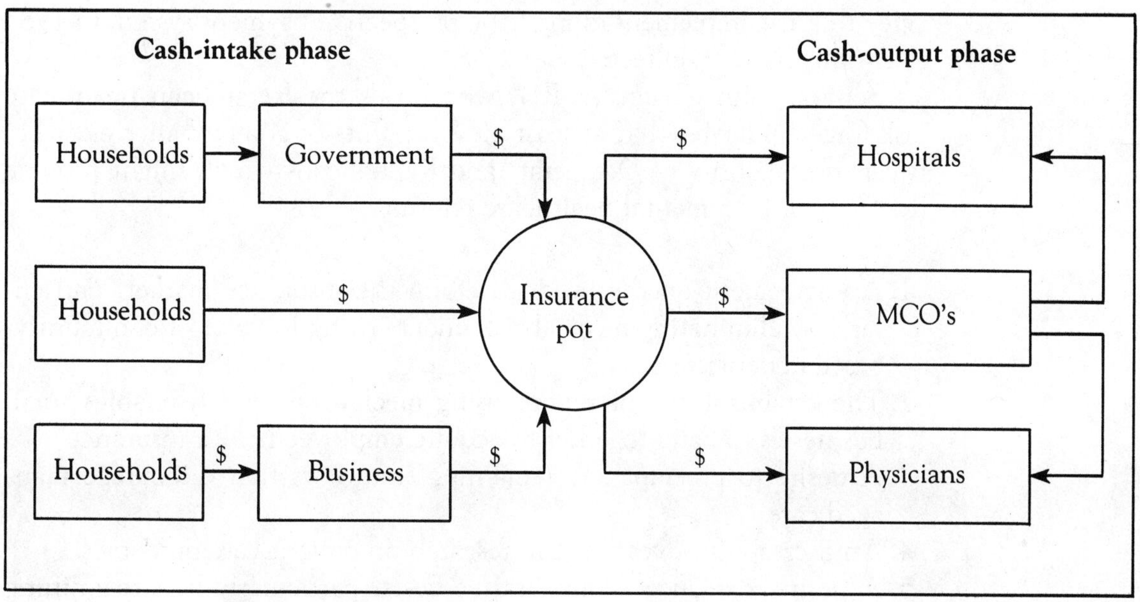

Figure 1-2 Cash flow stream as described by the Clinton administration's healthcare reform proposal

- *Indigent families.* The government would subsidize their premiums based upon their level of income.

Choice of Doctors

To some extent the ability to select a private physician will still be available, but people will be encouraged to join managed care groups that may limit their choice of doctors.

Other Reforms

The Clinton plan also calls for improved health education programs in schools and workplaces, more rural and inner-city health clinics to provide better access to primary care at the community level, education reforms to encourage physicians to become primary care providers, and more training for certified nurse midwives and nurse practitioners. It also has been suggested that the Medicare program be expanded to include improved long-term care coverage, with an emphasis on home-based and community-based care.

Incremental Reform

If agreement on comprehensive healthcare reform is not achieved, a number of points of commonality between Democrats and Republicans may provide the basis for incremental changes to the current system. A number of legislators in both parties have indicated a distaste for incremental reform, believing that the implementation of such reform simply provides an opening for additional cost shifting. A number of policymakers now agree that the implementation of the prospective payment system in 1983 essentially had this efffect.

Senator John Chafee (R-RI), who heads the Republican healthcare task force, indicates that at least eleven points of commonality exist between the majority of Democrats and Republicans which might provide the basis for incremental healthcare reform:

1. An agreement on the need to reform the insurance market, particularly by eliminating medical risk underwriting in favor of community-based underwriting
2. The establishment of a purchasing mechanism which enables small businesses to band together to acquire employee health insurance
3. A desire to preempt any remaining state laws that discourage managed care
4. An increase in investment in research on patient care outcomes
5. A desire to reduce administrative costs, particularly by streamlining the utilization review process for most providers

6. Increased investment in community health centers
7. Encouragement of the use of primary and preventive care
8. The need to increase the ability of states to obtain waivers under Medicaid
9. The need to achieve equity in the tax code by granting 100 percent deductibility for self-employed individuals, who today can deduct only 25 percent of their healthcare benefits for tax purposes
10. A desire to preempt state-mandated health benefits
11. A desire to expand Medicare funding for preventive care

Managed Care Data Base

In the near future another organization may be set up to review managed care plans and providers. Work is under way to develop a national data base that will enable consumers and businesses to evaluate managed care plans. The plans will be rated in terms of their preventive services, prenatal care, and management of chronic conditions. Data will also be collected on surgical outcomes and patient satisfaction. The initiative is supported by a coalition of thirty major managed care companies that cover more than 55 million subscribers and by large corporations such as Xerox, General Electric, and Hewlett-Packard.

Healthcare Spending

Figure 1-3 shows increases and decreases in the types of healthcare services being rendered and percentage differences in where money is being spent.

Threats, Opportunities, and Strategies for Private Practices

In all likelihood, an increasing percentage of patients and organizations will move their health insurance coverage from traditional indemnity insurance to managed care plans (HMOs, preferred provider organizations, exclusive provider organizations, etc.). Employers are aggressively looking for methods to reduce insurance expenses without reducing levels of coverage for their employees. A popular alternative for employers is managed care. What impact will this have, and what can practices expect in the future? A heavy burden has been placed on the shoulders of physicians and practices to provide quality care at a lower cost. This new responsibility has created threats as well as opportunities for the medical practice of the 1990s.

Threats

A managed care plan typically restricts the physician's latitude in caring for patients. The utilization protocol of a managed care company may

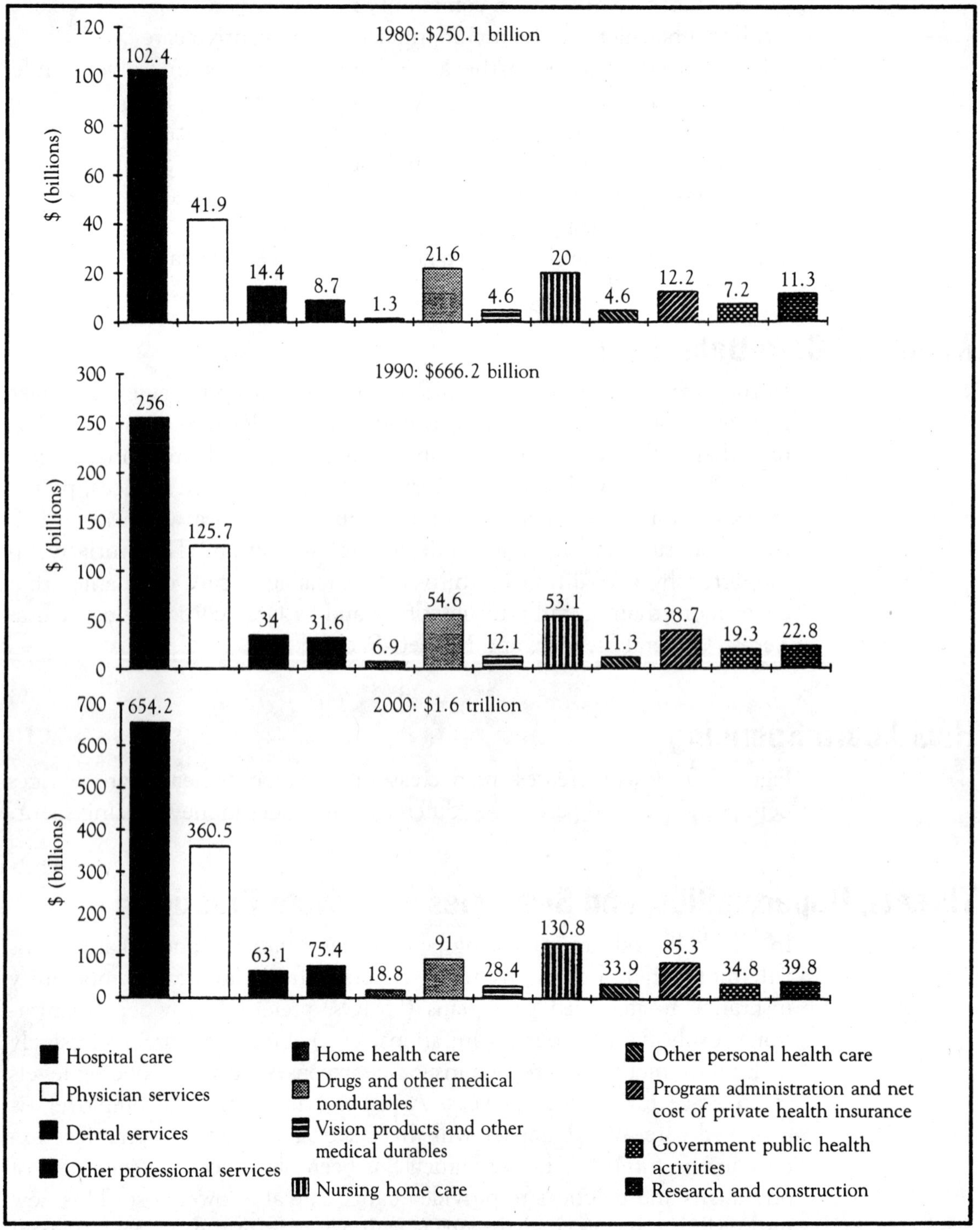

Figure 1-3 Projected Changes in Healthcare Costs (*From the Healthcare Financing Administration*).

strongly suggest a plan of treatment different from the plan preferred by the treating physician. This situation could increase the likelihood of a malpractice suit being brought against that physician. Under popular capitation contracts, physicians can also be faced with a substantial financial risk from *incurred but not recorded (IBNR)* medical claims when their patients are referred to other healthcare providers. The physician has to rely on the managed care carrier to provide sufficient, accurate, and timely information to assess the potential for a sizable adjustment to future capitation payments or IBNR adjustments to the physician's capitation payments. The physician also runs the risk of adverse selection by enrollees of the managed care company. This can have an impact on the physician's practice in two ways. First, these members can require an extraordinary amount of the physician's time, precluding him or her from treating higher-paying fee-for-service patients. Second, these members could require additional services that could be charged against the money capitation payments or the reduced-risk pool.

Managed care companies can create an increased administrative burden on a physician's office. Examples include incompatible claim systems, the need for authorization before providing care, required physician interaction with utilization review departments, required quality assurance reporting, and increased analysis to review periodic reports provided by managed care companies (e.g., determination of IBNR exposure and detection of inappropriate charges against the provider's risk pool or capitation). Finally, a managed care company may require participating physicians to carry additional malpractice insurance.

Opportunities

Why have so many doctors contracted with managed care companies when this exposes a physician to so many threats?

1. A managed care company often provides greater exposure to a healthcare provider, becoming a marketing arm for a physician.
2. All physicians are included in a provider directory which is circulated to all the members of a managed care plan.
3. Usually, the physicians listed in these directories gain an increased patient load.
4. An increased patient load usually results in greater revenue to the physician, and revenue usually becomes more predictable.
5. Physician referrals are often increased as most managed care companies either require the use of providers listed in the directory or provide increased reimbursement incentives to patients for using those providers.
6. Typically, managed care benefits provided to patients are more comprehensive (including preventive care), reducing overall medical costs.

Strategies

How can an individual practice weigh the opportunities against the disadvantages of contracting with a managed care company? A practice must strategically assess its position and market influences. Is there excess capacity for additional patients, or will the physicians be displacing current fee-for-service patients with managed care patients expected? If no excess capacity exists, should the physicians add another physician or physician extenders to the practice to accommodate the additional patients expected? How does the reimbursement rate of the managed care plan compare with the physician's existing fee structure? If the practice becomes a plan provider, will this induce existing fee-for-service patients to join the plan? How will joining a managed care plan affect the practice's administrative load? Will there be a need to increase the staff? Are the utilization review and the quality assurance procedures compatible with the physicians' style of practice? How will salaries and methods of income distribution be changed? If there is a capitation arrangement, who will analyze the utilization report to determine the following:

1. Existing exposure from the IBNR claims charged
2. Inappropriate claims against a physician (duplicate claims for any other provider's patients)
3. More efficient ways to provide care for the patient

Seeking Outside Assistance

If a practice decides that outside assistance is needed from a consultant, the adviser should pass a strict qualifications and credentials review, including the following:

1. Knowledge of prominent managed care plans in the community
2. Knowledge of the subscriber/patient base of local managed care plans
3. Knowledge of private practice finances to assess a practice's position as it relates to insurance and managed care
4. Knowledge of and experience with physician joint ventures and networking
5. Ability and past experience in negotiating managed care contracts

The healthcare consultant's experience in and familiarity with these areas will help the practitioner identify opportunities for expanding through marketing and achieving cost reductions and productivity gains in the daily management of the practice. It also will maximize cash flow through improvements in billing and collections and diversify a physician's income through participation in sound medical and related business ventures. Ideally, the healthcare industry should be able to contribute a broad business perspective in identifying the opportunities which may be available to an individual practice.

CHAPTER 2

Types of Managed Care Plans

The Future of Managed Care

Managed care plans are not going to vanish. In fact, some healthcare analysts predict that 80 percent of the healthcare market will be controlled by managed care organizations (MCOs) by 1995. Practices that ignore the existence of MCOs may be committing professional suicide because some of these plans may have enough specialists in a practice's specialty by the time that practice wants to sign on. If MCOs are closed to new providers with a given specialty and if a majority of a practice's patients are insured through an MCO, payment to that practice may be severely reduced. The rules of healthcare reimbursement have changed, and those who recognize, understand, and react to this change will gain a competitive advantage.

Increased Interest in Managed Care

According to the seventh annual *HealthCare Benefits Survey* by A. Foster Higgins, the average healthcare cost per employee exceeded $3900 in 1992. The growth of managed care plans is due in part to spiralling health insurance costs and lack of control of utilization under traditional fee-for-service plans in which providers are reimbursed under a usual, customary, and reasonable (UCR) payment vehicle. While managed care plans do not stop increases in healthcare expenditures, most studies, including this one, have found that they hold such increases down. According to the survey,

30% of employers offer only managed care plans to their employees. Another reason for the interest in managed care plans is that they increase competition between physicians, thereby driving down costs.

At present managed care plans are most common in California and the midwest. Lower penetration has been found in the mountain regions and in New England. Penetration of health maintenance organizations (HMOs) specifically is down in the midwest, south central and mountain regions but up in the west, south Atlantic, mid-Atlantic and New England regions. No regional data are available with regard to the penetration of other types of plans.

The main obstacle to growth in rural and small town areas is geography. Most networks of doctors and hospitals currently work in major metropolitan areas.

Impact on Physicians

The prevalence of managed care indicates that physicians will be forced to accept such plans as a fact of life. As an increasing number of doctors become contract physicians with MCOs, competition for key plans will rise. Also, the ability to contract successfully with MCOs will become a critical factor in a practice's success.

The executive vice president of the American Medical Association (AMA), Dr. James Todd, acknowledged at a 1992 meeting of the Group Health Association of America (GHAA), the main association of managed care organizations, that while the AMA has long recognized the existence of MCOs, it has been slow to recognize and accept the benefits of HMOs. He noted that organized medicine's opposition to HMOs dates back to the early 1900s, when local medical societies tried to prevent their members from participating in organized prepaid health plans. Dr. Todd also acknowledged the positive contributions made by HMOs.

Patients' View of Managed Care Plans

When insureds consider joining an MCO, they typically struggle with the idea of changing physicians. In an MCO, the out-of-pocket expense incurred by the enrollee is usually lower than is the case with traditional indemnity plans. Some patient satisfaction surveys show that insureds who have had both a fee-for-service insurance plan and an MCO plan prefer the MCO. The jury is still out on insureds' preferences for MCOs over traditional indemnity plans.

Focus on Quality

In the near future health insurance will probably place greater emphasis on quality in conjunction with cost. Medical insurance has become so expensive that employers and individuals purchasing insurance on the basis of price alone. Some studies indicate that quality of care will become increasingly important. A study conducted by Opinion Research Corp., a subsidiary of Arthur D. Little, found that employees in a large Atlantic Coast state would be willing to pay higher out-of-pocket for what they perceive as better care.

While quality is currently defined in basic terms such as waiting time to see a physician, morbidity and mortality rates, and difficulty in obtaining a specialty referral, some analysts of the healthcare industry forecast that quality soon will be measured by criteria such as time spent with the patient and the clinical outcomes. Physicians may be assigned quality ratings by hospitals, managed care groups, and the government. Some managed care plans already provide financial rewards to doctors with high ratings, just as they offer incentives to cost-efficient primary care physicians in the form of returning withholds.

If quality becomes more important to insureds, managed care plans will attempt to measure, document, and market it. In fact, this is already happening in that some MCOs use clinical relapse rates in choosing mental health providers. An increased emphasis on quality could make an MCO very choosy about the practitioners it invites to become members. (The largest publicly held HMO, U.S. Healthcare, is already picky about the providers it accepts. Physicians must schedule no more than five patients per hour, keep medical records that adhere to U.S. Healthcare's standards, and provide twenty-four-hour service.) MCOs will probably be able to contact Medicare and Medicaid to learn of possible fraud and abuse penalties before accepting a practitioner, and peer review data may be scrutinized more carefully.

Strategies Utilized By Managed Care Organizations

Specific strategies used today by MCOs to control costs include preauthorization of necessity (prospective review); concurrent review during hospital stays; quality management programs; utilization review, frequently using peer review organizations (PROs); diagnosis-related group (DRG) payments to hospitals, skilled nursing facilities, and home healthcare agencies; second opinions; case management; patient outcomes research; and computerized prepayment edits.

Following are a few definitions of some of the terms:

Quality management, (QM) includes not only monitoring treatment type and duration for inpatient stays but retrospective review (review of the necessity and appropriateness of treatment after it has been rendered).

Quality management also can include

- Sanctions for doctors who fail to comply
- Provider education and a notification/feedback system
- Patient education and a wellness-orientation program
- Patterns of care norms for the community
- Clear documentation by the physician

Prepayment edits ensure that a private practice has not fragmented services (also referred to as *unbundling*), rendered services too frequently, or provided services not substantiated by the diagnosis.

Among these strategies, the one that affects physicians the most if more services are rendered in the office than in the hospital is prepayment edits. Dr. Gail Wilensky, former head of HCFA, considers "a la carte coding" by practitioners one of the biggest problems in the Medicare Part B program.[1] HCFA is addressing the issue through the development of more prepayment edits for Medicare claims.

So-called double-dipping is the practice of reporting two and three codes to represent the services a physician rendered instead of reporting the single larger procedure code that includes the lesser services. This is an area that has recently received much attention in the lay press, which often makes it look like a common practice, when in fact the number of practitioners who unbundle is small. Many health insurance industry publications estimate that unbundling occurs most frequently in OB/GYN and orthopedic specialties. The ability of payers, whether they are managed care plans or indemnity plans with some elements of managed care in place, to identify inappropriate coding through the use of software will in all likelihood improve, according to industry analysts. Also, specialty societies may develop policies on what should be bundled versus what services should be reported separately. Some specialty societies, such as the American Academy of Orthopedic Surgeons, have already done so.

Another managed care strategy that will affect services in the office setting as much as it will inpatient services is the use of claims data to identify low-quality or inefficient providers and establish a standard for practices that are asked to remain in a managed care organization.

Healthcare insurance analysts also forecast that managed care will evolve to use strategies that integrate finance, administration, and delivery, largely at the request of employers who contract with MCOs for these controls.

Growth of Managed Care Organizations

Future growth will lie with point-of-service (POS) plans as a result of their ability to combine many of the best features of other approaches. Physician Administrative Organizations, (PAOs) also are likely to grow. Undoubtedly, Medicaid and workers' compensation managed care plans will become more prevalent if they are not rolled into a larger federal program. Medicare will probably remain the same until 1996 but may move further into the managed care arena in 1997. In fact, Medicare managed care plans have grown and cost savings with these alternatives have already been realized.

[1] *Medical Economics*, "What's Ahead in Payment Reform and Practice Controls?", June 15, 1992, p.164.

While there are many proposals before Congress for healthcare reform, inaction remains while the Clinton administration formulates its recommendations. If Congress and the administration enact some healthcare reform measures, they will probably not be implemented for at least a year and it is likely that the final legislation will contain some elements of managed care.

In terms of the strategies that will be used to control costs, it is likely that preauthorization for outpatient services (already prevalent with inpatient services) will be required. The tracking of outcomes data also may become more predominant.

The impact of the growth of managed care on private practitioners will include fewer solo practices as many practices become larger to reduce overhead costs and to have stronger negotiating power with MCOs. Office managers and practice administrators will have to develop more sophisticated skills to deal with the various aspects of the business.

Plans

The widely used term *managed care* refers to techniques as well as organizations that depend on cost-effective healthcare. While no strict definition is available, this term is defined by many insurance industry analysts and healthcare providers to include HMOs, Preferred Provider Organizations (PPO), (POS) or negotiated provider agreements, and even indemnity plans that rely on utilization review or another third party as the bedrock of their administration. These different varieties of MCOs intervene between a patient and a physician in order to determine, on behalf of the patient, what would be a necessary or appropriate course of treatment. This is achieved by the MCO setting limits on benefit payments, services, and/or providers. Typically, comprehensive benefits are provided through a managed or coordinated care plan, but managed care may be applied to limited services such as dental or mental care.

Perhaps managed care can be defined most succinctly as care that is managed in part by an entity other than the doctor or patient, typically an insurer or employer.

The proponents of managed care maintain that few patients can make an intelligent choice about medical care and that with the payor traditionally playing no role, the normal market forces that tend to hold down prices have been absent from the healthcare field. Involving the payor in these decisions should impose cost restraints.

Frequently, private practitioners are not fond of the loss of autonomy that can occur with managed or coordinated care plans. Specifically, doctors do not like playing "Mother, may I?" with MCOs. Other sentiments expressed by physicians are that MCOs change referral relationships and thus cause the private practice fee to become fictional, waste staff time in obtaining preauthorization, and adversely affect patient care if the doctor is paid a flat yearly fee.

Nevertheless, private practitioners feel "forced" to join MCOs to maintain or increase their practice base. The AMA estimates that 50 percent of its members are affiliated with one or more managed care plans. Many physicians feel compelled to contract with MCOs because they believe that they may not have the option of becoming involved later if some MCOs are "closed" to practitioners of their specialty.

The term *coordinated care,* as opposed to managed care, is being used more frequently. Health insurance executives tout this term because they maintain that care cannot be managed successfully unless it is coordinated. They contend that the term *managed care* can be misconstrued by the patient, whereas *coordinated care* has a better connotation. For the purposes of this book, the term *managed care* will be used to describe both coordinated care and managed care, since the difference is largely one of semantics.

Sources of Information on Managed Care Organizations

The GHAA, the industry group for MCOs, maintains a listing of HMOs that are federally qualified, lists of numbers of insureds by plan and contact persons at each plan, a list of MCOs that are members of the GHAA, and other helpful data. The GHAA can be reached in Washington, D.C., at (202)778–3200. Psychiatrists can obtain a list of managed mental healthcare plans in the June 8, 1992 issue of *Business Insurance*, (vol. 26, no. 23).

Definitions

Familiarity with the different types of MCOs on the part of physicians, insurance personnel, and managers is crucial in determining whether to join one or more MCOs. The following definitions and information regarding the varying MCOs can be helpful in this regard.

Direct contracting: done by large employers that contract directly with healthcare providers. By eliminating the middleman (insurer), these employers usually lower the cost of insuring their employees and their family members. Direct contracting is currently more prevalent with hospitals than with independently practicing physicians.

Exclusive Provider Organization (EPO): a hybrid HMO that utilizes a closed network of providers and a primary care gatekeeper. One difference between an EPO and a PPO is that only a certain number of doctors in each specialty are allowed in an EPO, whereas a PPO typically does not have such a cap. Also, unlike an HMO, an EPO plan is often self-funded by the employer. When serving self-insured employers, it has the advantage of avoiding state benefit mandates such as preventive care. In certain cases EPOs typically are experience-rated (rates are determined by the actual cost of delivering medical care to only the company's employees) instead of community-rated (rates are based on averages for the entire MCO enrollment). Most HMOs are community-rated.

Health Maintenance Organization (HMO): a prepaid health program of group practices, with comprehensive medical care typically provided. Often there is an emphasis on preventive medicine.

There are many different kinds of HMOs. The most traditional may be called a *closed-panel* HMO, in which a group of doctors usually work exclusively for a single organization, frequently a large one with strong marketing skills. In most instances HMOs have primary care gatekeepers so that a patient cannot see a specialist without first having seen the gatekeeper and obtaining authorization for evaluation or treatment by a specialist; this is done for cost-containment purposes.

HMOs use a capitated form of reimbursement more often than other MCOs do. With a capitation vehicle, the medical practice agrees to provide a stated range of services for a fixed price. The price paid does not vary with the scope, risk, intensity, or frequency of services provided. The risks assumed by the practitioners are consequently greater with capitation agreements than in discounted fee-for-service arrangements.

HMOs can be of varying models, including staff, group, network, and independent practice associations. For example, a *staff model* HMO brings all the disciplines under one roof through a multispecialty clinic that offers a restrictive choice of specialists but some freedom to change one's primary care physician. A staff model HMO can be either for profit or not for profit. In this type of HMO, the HMO often owns the hospital and employs the physicians; an example would be Kaiser Permanente.

In a *medical group* HMO, (1) the employer decides to build its own HMO as an integral part of the organization or (2) the employer develops a separate HMO corporation which contracts with a medical group or clinic for medical services for the employees.

In a *network-based* HMO, the HMO contracts with two or more multispecialty clinics to treat the bulk of its patients. This type of HMO has quality assurance committees, medical record committees, medical review committees, and other appropriate standards groups, all composed of physicians who are members of that network. Good programs (from the viewpoint of the insurance industry) also collect information on individual physician practice patterns and provide the appropriate feedback.

HMOs must have, according to many industry estimates, 20,000 to 50,000 enrollees, depending on the model, to achieve a stable positive net income.

Current estimates indicate that approximately 15 percent (32 million) of insureds belong to HMOs. While this type of managed care product was the first managed care option (established first in California with Kaiser Permanente) and enrollment grew in the 1970s and early 1980s at a rate of 20 to 25 percent, the growth of HMOs has slowed more recently to about 10 percent. Perhaps the interest in HMOs has waned in some areas because many benefit specialists have found that HMOs do not control costs as well as other types of managed care plans do. Higher utilization of healthcare services occurs frequently in some HMOs; this is often as a result of a small copay, as little as $3 in some cases. This also may have contributed to the slower growth of HMOs.

Independent Practice Association (IPA): a separate legal entity that (1) organizes physicians to contract with HMOs to provide physician services or (2) actually becomes an HMO and services its enrollees.

In the first arrangement, the IPA is a partnership or association that is a physician management organization, receiving payments (usually capitations) from the health plan and arranging for or delivering medical services. Contracts are drawn between the HMO and the IPA that describe these payments, the services to be provided, and the nature of the peer review. The IPA then contracts with local physicians to provide care.

The second type of IPA model is now occurring with greater frequency since the federal HMO office recognizes it as a legitimate model that meets federal regulations. Instead of existing as two entities, the health plan and the IPA are merged. Independent physicians participate with the IPA/HMO on a fee-for-service basis by accepting the IPA's fee schedule with a risk holdback of 20 to 30 percent, just as they do in the first IPA arrangement. This model allows for simplification of design and economical management.

IPAs typically adopt the philosophy of offering comprehensive healthcare of other HMOs, with particular emphasis on appropriate primary preventive services but with enrollee choice of both the physician and the location in which services will be rendered. Physicians have an equity interest in the IPA.

Physician Administrative Organization (PAO): As with an IPA, doctors have an equity interest. A PAO has its own independent management or holding company that conducts business for the physician shareholders or partners. This arrangement allows the doctor to negotiate forcefully for the type and amount of reimbursement, formulate and administer quality and utilization guidelines, perform credentialing and peer review, and even own a hospital. A PAO sometimes procures supplies for the practice or negotiates for malpractice rates. Most prevalent in the western states, PAOs are predicted to become prominent in most metropolitan areas in the next eight to ten years. Doctors often speak highly of these plans because they allow for more autonomy than do other MCOs.

Physician Hospital Organization (PHO): involves the alignment of primary care doctors and hospitals. To achieve the linkage between primary care physicians (PCPs) and hospitals, PHOs have been formed to enable hospitals to utilize the PCP gatekeeper approach as they attempt to secure contracts for PCPs. The PHO allows providers to regain or retain the control that is often relinquished to another type of MCO. The PCPs provide a utilization review function, case management, and quality assurance and serve as gatekeepers, while the hospital provides the facility, the necessary capital, information gathering, and organizational expertise. Although direct contracting with industry is possible with this structure, a PHO can also contract with HMOs or PPOs (see *direct contracting*). The greatest strength of a PHO is the flexibility that allows it to provide for the specific and unique needs of an organization and to change methods and procedures as necessary to allow long-term partnerships with local employers.

Although some large HMOs own their own dedicated hospitals, many HMOs and PPOs select specific hospitals in covered areas and negotiate special rates for their members. Separate negotiations between large industries and hospitals have bypassed PPOs and HMOs entirely in some instances. This direct approach falters when a hospital cannot get the active involvement of physicians in the negotiations. In many instances physicians are indirectly in competition with hospitals. Independent ambulatory surgery centers, physician-owned laboratories, physical therapy diagnostic centers, and even birthing centers thrived under the ownership and management of physicians during the 1980s.

Point-Of-Service plan (POS): a hybrid between a traditional HMO and a PPO. In a POS plan, the insured is encouraged to seek medical care in a preferred provider network with a gatekeeper but care may be obtained outside the network at reduced coverage levels and at a higher cost. Often the copay for seeking care outside of the network is 30 percent. A POS feature might be included as a part of any MCO's offerings.

Most industry studies have found that POS growth has exceeded that of both HMOs and PPOs. One reason for this is that POS patients have the freedom to choose a provider. Approximately 11 percent of employers offered POS plans in 1991. Some industry analysts forecast that POS plans will bring managed care into the mainstream of health insurance.

Preferred Provider Organization (PPO): form of healthcare delivery in which a group of healthcare providers agrees to supply services to a defined group of patients at an agreed-on discounted fee-for-service rate; the rate varies considerably, but typically there is a discount of 15 to 20 percent. PPOs, unlike HMOs, allow patients to go out of the network for care, but with a higher copay. As a rule, PPOs are less restrictive than HMOs. One of the biggest differences is that HMOs finance and provide services or arrange for delivery whereas PPOs only provide services. Another difference is that HMOs, if federally qualified, are more regulated (through the HMO Act of 1973 and its amendments and through state legislation) than are PPOs, which are regulated only in a small number of states and are not subject to federal legislation.

Practitioners must be aware of the greater potential for restraint of trade, antitrust, and price-fixing implications with PPOs compared with HMOs. Such issues may arise when a PPO includes all or a major portion of the providers in an area. HMOs avoid most antitrust problems by offering alternative insurance packages along with alternative physicians to the insured.

Utilization Review Organizations (UROs): An organization which performs the process by which decisions on hospital admissions are examined in advance by an external reviewer. This reviewer is accountable to an employer, insurer, HMO, PPO, IPA, or other entity responsible for all or most of the cost of care.

The utilization review process assesses the medical appropriateness of a suggested course of treatment for a particular patient. This system provides the patient and the payer with some assurance of the appropriateness, value, and quality of healthcare services. The most common form of utilization review is preadmission certification, a process by which the attending physician or the patient requests approval for any nonemergency admission to an inpatient facility.

Medicaid Managed Care Plans

According to HCFA statistics, 10 percent of the nation's Medicaid population is enrolled in managed care networks in thirty states. The percentage of Medicaid recipients enrolled in a managed care plan increased in the period from June 1989 to June 1990 by 19 percent, HCFA states. HCFA would like to see that number grow, especially since Medicaid managed care networks are proving to be cost-efficient, saving more than $225 million in the last two years. Since HCFA estimates that Medicaid managed care plans can deliver better, more balanced care for 5 percent less, the growth of these managed care plans undoubtedly will continue.

Most Medicaid managed care programs offer PCPs a fixed monthly fee to provide care to a fixed Medicaid population. To determine if Medicaid offers a managed care program in the area where a practice is located, one can contact Medicaid or the regional HCFA office in that area (Figure 2-1).

Since Medicaid is financed through state programs which utilize matching federal funds, HCFA has attempted to shape many of these state programs by withholding matching funds or encouraging the development of particular programs. There is a greater amount of state flexibility permitted in efforts to change methods and develop new ones. Along with those changes, greater restrictions on patients' freedom of choice has occurred.

Arizona offered the first statewide Medicaid managed care program in 1982, although this plan is still considered a demonstration project and must receive special congressional approval to continue. Oregon has proposed perhaps the most innovative Medicaid plan: Approximately 700 diagnoses (conditions) have been listed in order from most to least serious. The proposed Oregon program may, if legislated, fund only 650 of the 700 conditions, depending on the funds available. Thus, recipients may not receive treatment for conditions, such as a cold, for which there is no real treatment. While appeals are still being considered, the proposal in Oregon has not been approved because it conflicts with the Americans with Disabilities Act (ADA).

Workers' Compensation Managed Care Plans

Managed care vendors are expanding their networks to meet the demands of employers who want to apply managed care strategies to control work-

REGION I: Maine, Vermont, New Hampshire, Massachusetts, Connecticut, Rhode Island
John F. Kennedy Federal Bldg.
Room 1309
Boston, MA 02203
Sydney Kaplan
(617) 565-1188

REGION II: New York, Puerto Rico, Virgin Islands
26 Federal Plaza
Room 3811
New York, NY 10278
William Toby
(212) 264-4488

REGION III: Pennsylvania, Maryland, Delaware, Virginia, New Jewsey, District of Columbia
3535 Market Street
Philadelphia, PA 19104
Maurice Hartman
(215) 596-1351

REGION IV: North Carolina, South Carolina, Kentucky, Tennessee, Mississippi, Alabama, Georgia, Florida
101 Marietta Tower Suite 701
Atlanta, GA 30323
Clarance J. Boone, Acting Regional Admin.
(404) 331-2329

REGION V: Minnesota, Wisconsin, Michigan, Illinois, Indiana, Ohio, West Virginia
105 W. Adams
15th floor
Chicago, IL 60603
Chester Stroyney
(312) 886-6432

REGION VI: Texas, New Mexico, Oklahoma, Arkansas, Louisiana
1200 Main Tower Building
Room 2000
Dallas, TX 75202
Ed Lessard, Act. Reg. Admin.
(214) 767-6428

REGION VII: Kansas, Missouri, Iowa, Nebraska
Federal Office Building
Room 235
601 East 12 Street
Kansas City, MO 64106
Gene Hyde
(816) 426-5233

REGION VIII: Colorado, Utah, Wyoming, South Dakota, North Dakota, Montana
Federal Building
1961 Stout Street Room 574
Denver, CO 80294
Frank Ishida, Act. Reg. Admin.
(303) 844-2111

REGION IX: California, Nevada Arizona, Hawaii, Guam, Samoa
75 Hawthorne Street
4th floor
San Francisco, CA 94105
Gerald M. Moskowitz
(415) 744-3502

REGION X: Washington, Oregon, Idaho, Alaska
2201 Sixth Avenue
Mail Stop RX40
Seattle, WA 98121
Nancy Dapper
(206) 442-0425

Figure 2-1 HCFA Regional office addresses

ers' compensation costs. Workers' compensation has been called the last bastion of fee-for-service, but it is a natural fit for managed care.

One large vendor (the Travelers Insurance Company) recently expanded its network to provide managed care services for workers' comp cases and operate workers' comp PPOs in thirty-one states. Travelers and many other workers' comp managed care plans feature a toll-free twenty-four-hour hot line that enables an employer to report an injury quickly enough that appropriate care can begin immediately. Physicians who treat patients with on-the-job injuries (orthopedists, physiatrists, etc.) may want to join a Workers' Compensation MCO, particularly if they are trying to increase their patient base. Other insurers offering workers' comp MCOs include Aetna and Private Healthcare Systems, Inc., although the workers' option is not offered by these carriers in every area.

Some large employers have contracted directly with hospitals and physicians for workers' compensation rather than working through an insurer. Although some state laws prohibit employers from directing an employee to a provider, some employers in those states contend that state laws permit them to say to the employee, "See this physician first."

Medicare and Managed Care

Medicare got involved in HMOs in 1982. A new financial incentive was added for managed care HMOs, a risk-related contract which allowed an HMO to keep the savings it could achieve in the management of care; previously, HMOs were allowed to keep only 10 percent of the savings. The Medicare program has been very strong in establishing managed care as a result of congressional actions to hold down costs. Senior citizens' voting powers have inspired efforts to hold down the cost to the individual patient enrolled in Medicare.

Medicare's most pronounced efforts were made in 1983, when methods were changed for reimbursing hospital services through DRG-type reimbursements. This is a technique that bases reimbursement on the illness of the patient, forcing hospitals to distribute healthcare services or suffer in terms of profitability.

Parallel to these activities, different utilization and quality control review organizations were created to assure that as costs are held down, the quality of care will not be diminished. The original professional standards review organizations (PSROs) were replaced with PROs. Chartered PROs across the country conduct audits and review medical claims and examine utilization, peer review, and validation of DRG classifications.

In 1985 Congress recognized the need to lower costs for private practice physicians outside of hospitals. A Physician Payment Review Commission (PPRC) was created in 1986 to work on a multitude of approaches to lowering costs without diminishing services, and a law was passed in 1989 that changed the basis of physician reimbursement. The physician payment reform implemented on January 1, 1992, includes not only the fee schedule based on a resource-based relative value scale (RBRVS) but a host of controlling elements such as more bundling edits through HCFA's Correct Coding Initiative to keep costs from rising at the same pace.

Before the Tax Equity and Fiscal Responsibility Act (TEFRA) of 1982, Medicare's coverage was focused on either the few organizations that could meet the stringent requirements of the Public Health Service or the majority of HMOs that billed Medicare for individual services rendered rather than as prepayment organizations. Changes in TEFRA made it easier to deal with Medicare as a prepayment organization by including inducements for an organization to participate on a risk basis. Competitive medical plans (CMPs) may not meet legal HMO standards but still can provide services on a prepayment basis.

Many PPOs, HMOs, and other plans can more easily qualify as an eligible organization with CMP status. The assistant secretary of health makes a determination that an entity is an overqualified HMO or meets the definition of a CMP. After this determination, HCFA may enter into a contract with that organization. Eligibility requirements for an HMO to be HCFA-qualified include the following:

1. The organization must have sufficient administrative capacity.
2. It must have 5,000 enrollees or, if rural, 1,500 enrollees.
3. No more than 50 percent of the members can be Medicare/Medicaid.
4. It must have open enrollment periods at least thirty days a year.
5. It must demonstrate the ability to furnish the entire range of Medicare services available in the geographic area with the exception of hospice care.
6. It must assume financial responsibility and provide reasonable reimbursement for emergency services outside the organization.
7. In most instances services must be provided under the direct supervision of a physician. The services of physician assistants, nurse practitioners, and clinical psychologists may be provided in some cases without direct personal supervision.
8. The organization must ensure that services are accessible with reasonable promptness.
9. The organization must maintain a medical record system.
10. The organization must have quality assurance programs.
11. Physicians supervising patient care must be legally authorized to perform the service in the state.

Risk Reimbursement (Medicare HMOs and CMPs)

HMOs and CMPs may be reimbursed either on a risk basis or on a reasonable cost basis. Certain criteria must be met to qualify for risk-based reimbursement. Once it is qualified, an organization is paid in advance on a monthly per capita basis in accordance with a prescribed formula.

A key to the profitability of a Medicare HMO or CMP is the profitability that organization has with its non-Medicare enrollees. The adjusted community rate (ACR) is based on the premiums charged to non-Medicare enrollees, which are modified to allow for the specific services covered by Medicare and the expected Medicare patient's utilization. This ACR is compared to the average payment rate (APR), a precalculated rate that represents the typical costs of providing Medicare services in the area. When the APR is higher than the ACR, the difference is referred to as "savings." The savings can be used to build a benefit stabilization fund which will buffer patients from short-term fluctuations in the availability of additional benefits and also can be used to provide additional benefits or to lower the cost of deductibles or coinsurance. Currently, there are eighty-three risk-contracting HMOs or CMPs.

Cost Reimbursement (Medicare HMOs and CMPs)

Some organizations may not qualify for risk reimbursement or may choose not to participate. They may still participate in Medicare as an "eligible organization" as either an HMO or a CMP. A formula is used to predict costs and calculate payments by Medicare either directly to the organization or to hospitals and skilled nursing facilities separately. Payments made to a cost-basis organization are subject to a retroactive corrective adjustment at the end of each contract year.

Recent legislation (safe harbor rules published in the July 29, 1991, *Federal Register*) that prohibits financial gain from referring Medicare patients probably will limit the growth of these joint efforts between unrelated medical groups. The Office of the Inspector General has not come out with a complete statement with regard to managed care programs for Medicare beneficiaries; its position will continue to evolve. Very large groups such as hospitals and other structured organizations may consequently become the sole owners of these entities.

Approximately 2 million Medicare beneficiaries were enrolled in Medicare managed care programs as of February 1991. HCFA is exploring ways to increase the use of managed care under Medicare, including revising the Medicare HMO payment method, giving beneficiaries a rebate equal to one-third of the Medicare Part B premium, allowing Medicare risk-contract HMOs to contract exclusively with employers' retiree groups, and allowing Medicare HMOs to hold continuous open enrollment for new Medicare eligibles.

Physician Incentive Plans with Medicare/Medicaid Patients

Effective utilization control that identifies both under- and overutilization is essential for the efficient operation of prepaid healthcare organizations. The goal is to minimize overutilization of services to prevent unnecessary spending and to reduce the risk of unnecessary and intrusive procedures.

However, a prepaid healthcare organization also needs to assure that all medically necessary services are provided to protect its patients' health and prevent the need for more costly care later. In addition, if a prepaid healthcare organization inappropriately limits care, the organization may risk its reputation and jeopardize its ability to compete in the marketplace. Although professional ethics, risk of malpractice liability, and market competition help ensure the proper utilization of services, Medicare and Medicaid require both cost-reimbursed and risk organizations to have internal quality assurance programs, external quality review or medical audits, and other mechanisms to ensure the proper delivery of healthcare services.

Medicare and Medicaid contracts also are subject to periodic monitoring for compliance. In addition, the July 22, 1991, Notice of Proposed Rule Making on civil monetary penalties and intermediate sanctions provides for sanctions that may be imposed when an HMO or CMP fails to provide medically necessary services.

To encourage proper utilization, healthcare organizations offer a financial incentive as part of a physician incentive plan. Omnibus Budget Reconciliation Act of 1990, (OBRA '90) defines a physician incentive plan as "any compensation arrangement between an eligible organization and a physician or physician group that may directly or indirectly have the effect of reducing or limiting services provided with respect to individuals enrolled with the organization."[2]

Physicians in prepaid healthcare organizations generally receive fee-for-service payments, a salary, or capitation payments (a set dollar amount per patient) in return for the services they provide. Financial incentives may be used with the various types of physician payments to encourage appropriate levels of referral services. *Referral services* include any specialty, inpatient, outpatient, or laboratory services that a physician arranges but does not provide directly. Prepaid healthcare organizations may hold physicians or physician groups at risk for all or a portion of the cost of referral services so that they have a financial incentive to provide only medically necessary services. If the physician or physician group successfully controls the levels of referral services, it may receive additional compensation (an incentive payment) from the prepaid healthcare organization. The payment may take the form of unused capitation, a returned withhold, or a bonus payment.

1. A *capitation payment* is a set dollar amount per patient per month that a prepaid healthcare organization pays to a physician or physician group to cover a specified set of services without regard to the actual number of services provided to each enrollee. The capitation may cover the physician's services, referral services, or all medical services and/or administrative costs. If patient costs exceed the capitation amount, the physician must absorb the additional costs. If costs are below the capitation, the physician may keep the additional money.

[2] *Omnibus Budget Reconciliation Act of 1990*, P.L. 101—508.

2. *Withholds* are percentages of payments or set dollar amounts that a prepaid healthcare organization deducts from each physician or physician group's payment (salary, fees, or capitation). The amount withheld is set aside in pools to pay for specialty referral services and inpatient hospital services. The withhold may be used to pay for referral services. When referral costs exceed a prepaid healthcare organization's budget, part or all of the withhold may be forfeited, depending on the terms of the contract. If referral costs do not exceed the ceiling, part or all of the withhold may be returned to the physician or physician group. Some plans limit the amount of the risk to the withhold; others hold the physician or physician group liable for amounts beyond the sum withheld. Withholds are most often used with fee-for-service or capitation payments.

3. *Bonuses* are payments that prepaid healthcare organizations make to a physician or physician group beyond the set salary, fee-for-service payment, or capitation. Bonuses may be based on a physician or physician group's level of referral services or may be independent (e.g., based on the overall performance of the organization). This system is most often used for salaried physicians in staff model HMOs.

If the physician or physician group has excessive referrals, as defined by the prepaid healthcare organization, it may not receive incentive funds. In addition, the organization may hold the physician or physician group liable for referral costs that exceed a specified threshold. The healthcare organization may also increase the physician or physician group's withhold or make other changes in its incentive arrangements.

Many physician incentive plans incorporate *stop-loss protection* to limit the liability of the physician or physician group. Most often, the stop-loss protection limits a physician's maximum liability per patient to a specific dollar amount. For example, the organization may limit a physician's liability to $5,000 per patient from his or her withhold fund even if the actual charges are higher. In some cases prepaid healthcare organizations place an aggregate limit on the liability a physician can face. Instead of limiting liability to $5,000 per patient, the organization can limit total liability for all patients to $25,000. Stop-loss protection is particularly common with capitation arrangements.

Other variables may affect the amount of risk or the impact of financial incentives on physicians. For example, incentive payments may be calculated according to each individual physician's performance or according to a physician group's performance. The size of the physician group also affects the incentives. Performance may be evaluated over a long or a short period. The number of enrollees among whom the risk is spread and the amount of total income at risk vary. In addition, the relative health status of the patients involved increases the risk if the enrollees are high utilizers or may result in a lower level of risk if the enrollees are healthier than average. The percentage of the physician's practice that is made up of HMO/CMP patients as opposed to fee-for-service patients is also pertinent in this regard.

Stop-Loss Protection

By statute, HMOs and CMPs, that place physicians or physician groups at substantial financial risk for referral services provided to Medicare beneficiaries and Medicaid recipients must provide adequate and appropriate stop-loss protection. There are two levels of stop-loss protection, depending on the incentive plan's risk threshold. If the risk threshold is 25 percent (the incentive plan assesses or distributes payments no more often than annually), the stop-loss protection must protect physicians and physician groups from losses greater than 30 percent of the payments for the services they provide, plus payments for administrative costs and for controlling levels of referral services. If the risk threshold is 15 percent (the incentive plan assesses or distributes payments more often than annually), the stop-loss protection must protect physicians and physician groups from losses greater than 20 percent of payments.

In *capitated arrangements* it is difficult to determine prospectively what stop-loss would cover 30 percent of payments for services the physicians or physician groups provide, plus payments for administrative costs and for controlling levels of referral services. To make the stop-loss provisions for capitated arrangements comparable with the stop-loss provisions for bonus and withhold arrangements, no more than a 30 percent differential is permitted between the minimum and maximum payments a physician or physician group can receive. In other words, the difference between the maximum possible payments and the minimum possible payments can be no more than 30 percent of the maximum possible payments. If the incentive payments (or capitation) are paid more often than annually, the differential will be limited to 20 percent of the maximum payments.

These stop-loss levels are absolute limits on the physician or physician group's liability. The stop-loss protection must cover all referral costs over 20 or 30 percent of payments, depending on how frequently incentive payments are made. Liability above the stop-loss protection level may not be transferred to physicians or physician groups in later contract years. Since this protection limits total liability for all patients, it is referred to as an *aggregate liability limit*.

Many prepaid healthcare organizations design their stop-loss arrangements to limit liability for individual patients to a maximum dollar amount to protect against catastrophic cases. HCFA considered placing limits on a physician or physician group's maximum liability per patient instead of using a maximum aggregate liability limit. However, without an aggregate limit on liability, a physician or physician group could receive zero net payments from prepaid healthcare organizations.

Although individual stop-loss protection helps protect physicians and physician groups, a maximum limit on aggregate liability is necessary. Even if a physician group's liability is limited to no more then $10,000 per patient, if the group earns a good reputation for its treatment of AIDS patients, it could be liable for all its payments if increasing numbers of AIDS patients constitute the Medicare and Medicaid portion of the patient panel. Conceivably, the physician group would be forced to leave the prepaid healthcare organization, declare bankruptcy, or greatly restrict its treatment of all patients. Since it was Congress's intent to protect physicians and physician groups from unlimited liability, an aggregate limit is appropriate here.

Regardless of how the stop-loss protection is provided, the organization must assure HCFA or the states that all physicians or physician groups that provide services to Medicare beneficiaries and Medicaid recipients and are at "substantial financial risk" for referral services have stop-loss protection that meets the regulatory requirements.

Prohibited Physician Payments

As required by OBRA '90, regulations provide that physician incentive plans may operate only if no specific payment is made directly or indirectly under such a plan as an inducement to reduce or limit the medically necessary services provided to a specific enrollee. This provision specifically prohibits bonuses or other payments to a physician or physician group as an inducement to limit or reduce medically necessary services for any individual patient. Indirect payments include items of monetary value, such as waivers of debt and stock or equity in the organization. For example, an organization would be prohibited from paying a physician a $100 bonus or providing $100 of stock for each individual enrollee released from a hospital after the delivery of a child in two days versus three days if inpatient services were medically necessary on the third day. This does not prohibit all bonuses based on utilization. For example, bonuses that are based on general utilization levels (determined by aggregate patient utilization) are permitted.

Enforcement

Organizations that do not comply with these requirements may be subject to certain penalties. Determinations of noncompliance may result in civil monetary penalties, intermediate sanctions, and/or contract termination (for Medicare) or withholding of funds (for Medicaid). The civil penalties are limited to $25,000 for each determination of noncompliance. Under the intermediate sanctions provision, HCFA (for Medicare) or the state (for Medicaid) can suspend payment for new enrollees until it is satisfied that the basis for the determination is not likely to recur.

PRO Review of HMOs Under Medicare

PROs will continue to perform reviews of the quality of services, both inpatient and outpatient, furnished to Medicare enrollees by HMOs/CMPs with risk-based contracts. The major changes to the PRO contracts effective as of April 1993 are as follows:

1. There will be a standard "level" of review for all HMOs/CMPs. Previously, these plans were subject to three levels of review (limited, basic, and intensified) depending on the number or percentage of quality problems identified.
2. PROs will review a random sample of Medicare enrollees who have used HMO/CMP services, ranging from a minimum of 50 cases to a maximum of 300 per HMO/CMP, depending on Medicare enrollment size. PROs also will review a 10 percent random sample by HMO/CMP of deceased enrollees who used services during the twelve months before death and all beneficiary complaints regarding quality of care.
3. PROs will review twelve months of healthcare services for the cases selected in these random samples.
4. HMOs/CMPs will have sixty days rather than thirty days to provide the medical records required for review.
5. When quality concerns are identified through the PRO review process, the HMO/CMP and the PRO will cooperatively develop an action plan to correct those concerns. Under the previous contract, the follow-up action when problems were identified was an increase in the number of cases reviewed.
6. PROs will conduct a "targeted" review to demonstrate that quality concerns identified through their reviews have been corrected. Where appropriate, the review will focus on monitoring activities performed under the HMO/CMP's internal quality assurance plan.

CHAPTER 3

Is the Practice Ready?

Conducting an Analysis

A detailed analysis of the individual practice is a key component in evaluating the advantages of a managed care plan. The primary reason doctors sign managed care contracts usually is to increase or maintain market share. Frequently, a practice will make a hasty decision to join a managed care organization (MCO) because it has learned that a small percentage of its patients are leaving the practice to join that MCO, or new physicians who are establishing a practice may sign on with several new MCOs before performing the necessary calculations. However, it is not worth one's time to read, evaluate, and negotiate a contract if it will have little positive impact on a practice's patient base or does not have the potential to do so in the future.

Goal setting and strategic planning must be accomplished before a practice considers MCO participation. For example, the decision to join or not join an MCO will be much easier if the practice has considered important issues such as the following:

- What will the physician complement ultimately be (physician/staff size)?
- How many patients will the practice attempt to accommodate?
- Is there a desire to subspecialize and expand?
- Will satellite offices be established in the next five years?
- What marketing methods are acceptable and will be employed?

Patient Survey

The first step in assessing a practice's current position and arriving at a conclusion about which MCOs to join is the performance of a patient survey. The goal is to obtain patients' views of specific MCOs by asking a minimum of 200 patients the questions in Figure 3-1. Have patients complete the questionaire while waiting in the reception area:

After the patient survey has been conducted and the interest level of the current patients have been determined, a study should be conducted to assess the type of patients currently seen. This will assist the practitioner in negotiating contracts and decision making.

So that we may better serve our patients, we are trying to obtain our patients' perspective on managed care plans (HMOs, PPOs, etc.) in the area. To that end, we would appreciate your completing this questionnaire. Confidentiality is ensured. Please do not put your name on the questionnaire. When it is complete, please drop this questionnaire in the drop box at the front desk. Thank you in advance.

1. Please list the HMO and PPO plans in the area of which you are aware:

   ____________________ ____________________

   ____________________ ____________________

2. What, if any, unfavorable things have you heard about the plans listed above?

   ____

   ____

   ____

3. Which of the benefits offered (Preventive care, small copays, etc.) by HMOs, PPOs, and point-of-service plans are the most attractive to you? (If you are unfamiliar with these terms, please see the receptionist for an explanation).

   ____

   ____

   ____

4. Did you know that some managed care plans limit your choice of hospital and physician?

   Yes ________ No ________

5. Do you realize that some managed care plans discourage their physicians from referring patients to outside specialists and restrict the number of diagnostic tests that can be done?

   Yes ________ No ________

6. If you or your spouse is employed, does the employer currently offer you a managed care plan (such as an HMO, PPO, or point-of-service plan) as an alternative to other health insurance?

   Yes ________ No ________ Do not know ________

7. If you or your spouse is employed, what alternative plans does your employer offer you? Please list.

   ____________________ ____________________

8. Please provide information regarding your views of managed care plans by entering the appropriate number in the blanks below using this scale:

1	2	3	4	5
Strongly agree	Slightly agree	Neither agree nor disagree	Slightly disagree	Strongly disagree

   ________ a. I would not join a managed care plan.
   ________ b. I would seriously consider joining a managed care plan.
   ________ c. I would consider joining even if my doctor were not part of the plan.
   ________ d. I would consider joining only if this practice (*name practice*) decided to participate.

Thank you for your assistance. Your feedback will be carefully considered.

Figure 3-1. Patient managed care survey.

New Patients

List the average number of new patients in the last three years:

Last year ______ Year before last ______

% growth ______ % growth ______

Determining increases and decreases in new patients will help assess the need for joining a plan. Consider how many new patients the plan is expected to attract. Does the plan pay more for a new patient than for established patient? Look at whether there is appointment space available to absorb an increase in patients.

Record Transfer Request

How many patients have requested that their records be sent to another practice? This can indicate how many patients the practice may lose to an MCO.

	Last year	Year before last
Patient moving out of area	_____	_____
Patient enrolled in HMO (list)	_____	_____
______________________	_____	_____
______________________	_____	_____
______________________	_____	_____
Patient enrolled in a PPO (list)	_____	_____
______________________	_____	_____
______________________	_____	_____
______________________	_____	_____

Patient Demographics

Indicate the total number of patients seen in the last three years:

Last year	_____	Year before last	_____
% growth	_____	% growth	_____

List the age distribution of patients during the last year:

	Your practice	MCO
Under age 18 (break down further for a pediatric specialty)	_____	_____
18–34	_____	_____
35–49	_____	_____
50–64	_____	_____
65–74	_____	_____
75+	_____	_____

Check the type of employment that represents the patient base treated by the practice. Estimate the percentage each category represents.

	Your practice	MCO
Manufacturing, farming, construction	______	______
Service	______	______
Managerial/Professional	______	______
Self-employed	______	______
Business Owners	______	______
Retired	______	______

Compare the practice's patient demographics with a managed care plan's benefit structure, along with the populations targeted for marketing by the plan. Some age and sex categories utilize more healthcare and generate higher healthcare costs. Ask key questions such as the following: Does the reimbursement method take into consideration the case mix (how sick the patients are) and caseload (number of sick patients) of the practice? How was it calculated, and what base figures were used in the calculation? Ask the MCO for a copy of their calculation worksheet. Are the figures fair and appropriate? Are these the numbers the doctor would utilize to calculate reimbursement?

If the practice is not computerized, determine the number of active patients from ledger cards in a sampling of appointment books or the medical records' purging labels.

Some managed care plans vary capitation rates by patient ages. If the plan being considered does this, use the same age ranges that the plan uses when gathering data. Some specialists may need to divide the patient age mix into more categories. It is almost always beneficial to a practice to sign on with an MCO that bases capitation on age.

Active patient definitions will vary depending on medical specialties. Many practices consider an active patient one who has been seen at least once in the past three years.

Knowledge of the age and sex distributions and overall economic characteristics of active patients may be important in comparing the practice's demographics to that of employee groups in a particular plan.

Major Employers

While it is not practical to list all employers, it is helpful to include ten to twenty of the largest employers in the area. Consider asking the managed care company provide the practice with a list of major employer groups currently using their plans for use in making marketing projections. Contrasting this information with the employers of existing patients in the practice can enable one to determine how the contract may affect the practice's patient base. Knowledge of employers and the plans offered is paramount in determining how closely plan participation matches a practice's demographics. Employment information also is important in determining the likelihood of existing patients migrating to plans offered by employers and pinpointing patients who could be lost through nonparticipation in a particular system.

Where are the practice's patients employed, and what type of plan is offered?

Employer and plan	Number of patients	Percent of active patients
______________________	______	______
______________________	______	______
______________________	______	______

Referrals Made

Determine the total number of referrals from the practice to specialists in the last two years:

Last year ______ Year before last ______

% growth ______ % growth ______

List the four medical/surgical specialties to which patients are referred most frequently:

______________ ______________

______________ ______________

Referral data may be assessed by sampling a number of patients on the computer. Are these doctors members of the plan? If they are not, to whom are patients referred?

Specialty services are paid under capitation arrangements in some plans. Familiarity with referral patterns allows one to make a comparison with physician enrollees who fit practice patterns.

Often the definition of a primary care physician differs among plans. These definitions can affect reimbursement and contractual obligations.

Referrals Received

Indicate the total number of patients referred to the practice per year other than from managed care plans:

Last year ______ Year before last ______

% growth ______ % growth ______

List the sources of patient referrals to the practice (self, other patients; ancillary healthcare professionals, Yellow Pages advertisements, HMO, hospital physician referral service, etc.):

REFERRAL	SOURCE
______________	______________
______________	______________
______________	______________

Are those referral sources part of the plan; have they been approached about joining? What is the policy of the HMO/PPO?

Referral Income

What was the average referral income annually per patient:

Last year	______	Year before last	______
% growth	______	% growth	______

The impact that affiliation with a plan may have on a practice will be determined by how well the plan's physician affiliations resemble current referral patterns, reimbursement arrangements for referred patient care, and efficiency of the risk pools delivering quality health care. Are certain procedures reimbursed under a capitated rate, such as x-rays, lab and injections? Plan controls may interrupt patient care and patient trust as well as reduce income.

Referrals Affected

Determine which referrals may be affected by the plan. List the physicians most frequently referring patients who are members of the plan. List the physicians most frequently receiving referrals who are members of the plan.

Number of plan physicians to whom patients are regularly referred	Member physicians who regularly refer
______________	______________
______________	______________
______________	______________
______________	______________

The extent to which a plan resembles current referral patterns is a good measure of the suitability of that plan.

Many systems allow primary care physicians to perform certain predetermined procedures that are frequently handled by specialists and will allow reimbursement in accordance with specialist fee schedules. For each plan, the following questions should be addressed:

PLAN: ______________________________

CIRCLE ONE

Yes	No	Are there any referral restrictions in the contract?
Yes	No	Can physicians perform some procedures without a referral?
Yes	No	If so, must the doctors sign another contract?
Yes	No	If yes, how is the provider paid?
Yes	No	May patients self-refer to a specialist?
Yes	No	Are penalties assessed when referrals are made outside the plan?

Specialty Services

Can the doctor practice his or her specialty comfortably within the scope of the plan's limitations? For example, a psychiatrist who treats psychiatric disorders with long-term therapy may find that a managed care plan covers only short-term therapy. If the psychiatrist joined a managed care plan that covered only short-term therapy, he or she would be required to change his or her practice style significantly to make the contract financially worthwhile or treat few patients from the plan.

Volume of Services

Calculate the average number of visits per active patient per year (at least two years of data should be reviewed to identify changing trends or stability):

First year ______ Second year ______

Average visits can be determined by dividing total visits by the total number of active patients; average charges can be calculated by dividing the patient charges by the total number of patient visits.

Consideration of the average number of patient visits can assist a practice in predicting patient care needs and assist in determining the ability of the practice to care for all the patients in the plan. The average number of visits per patient is also needed to compute any capitation arrangements.

Learning which services are included under capitation rates and their frequency is necessary to forecast the effects of plan participation accurately. For example, are complete blood counts (CBCs) and other lab chemistry tests and projections routine, and are they covered under the proposed capitation?

Ancillary Service Costs

Indicate the average number and cost of in-office ancillary service units per patient per year. To obtain this information, it may be necessary to contact labs, therapists, etc., who provide outside lab services:

	Last year		Year before last	
Procedure	Number	Cost	Number	Cost
Laboratory	______	______	______	______
Spirometry	______	______	______	______
ECG	______	______	______	______
Allergy testing	______	______	______	______
Visual fields	______	______	______	______
Psychological testing	______	______	______	______
X-ray	______	______	______	______
Other diagnostic procedures:				
______________	______	______	______	______
______________	______	______	______	______
Other treatment procedures:				
______________	______	______	______	______
______________	______	______	______	______

Some managed care plans include these tests and procedures in capitation rates, while others allow the services to be billed using a predetermined fee schedule. This can lead to reductions in a practice's income.

The managed care plan may include some tests and procedures in the capitation rate for primary care physicians whether they are performed as part of the specialist's initial care or by the primary care physician. When specialists are required to send patients back to the primary care physician for ongoing monitoring or risk assumption, this can affect a "withhold pool."

Ancillary Service Claims

When reviewing a specific managed care plan, complete the following analysis of system treatment of ancillary services: Can ancillary services (lab, X ray, nurse practitioner, physician's assistant) be submitted to the MCO from the practice regardless of who provides the services? Must ancillary services be provided by a specific practice? Are there any supervisory requirements?

Ancillary care billed as fee for service		Specific requirements
Yes	No	______________
Yes	No	______________
Yes	No	______________

If a specific policy is necessary, the practice may find that it is working with many providers of the same service (for example, multiple radiologists of various plans). One should also consider whether the specified vendor renders services with a standard of practice that the physicians find acceptable.

Hospital Visits

What is the average reimbursement for hospital visits? Consideration of the amount of time spent with patients in the hospital is necessary to determine the capacity of a physician to see more patients. Some plans pay a set amount for hospital visits by specialty; others include hospital visits under capitation or surgery fees (for example, Medicare).

Private pay fee for hospital visits ______

Private pay fee for consults ______

Average number of hospital patient visits per week:

Last year	______	Year before last	______
% growth	______	% growth	______

Average number of consults per week:

Last year	______	Year before last	______
% growth	______	% growth	______

Average number of hospital procedures (diagnostic and surgical) performed per week:

Last year	______	Year before last	______
% growth	______	% growth	______

Computer Capabilities

Determine whether the practice's information system (either computer or ledger cards) will handle the increase in the patient load and track services and reimbursement as required by the MCO and/or as needed by the practice for appropriate monitoring.

Space

Is there adequate practice space to see additional patients?
Assessing the physician's ability or willingness to see more patients is vital in considering participation in a managed care plan. Some plans define the number of patients a physician may or must see (depending on how the physicians is paid for care). This number usually is expressed as a percentage of the total patients in a practice.

In practices where healthcare services may be provided by physician extenders (physician assistants, certified nurse practitioners, physical therapists, optometrists, etc.) it is important to determine a practice's capacity for all providers and whether the plan pays for those services as "incident to" or at a reduced rate.

Expansion

Will the practice need to buy or lease additional equipment or provide new procedures? List the standard services covered by the plan that are not part of routine office practice (physical exams for all patients and podiatric, psychological, optometric and chiropractic may all be required of primary care doctors in certain managed care plans). If the practice can not provide these services internally, does the contract permit it to arrange for such care through subcontractors?

This information may be subdivided according to inpatient and outpatient:

Treatment	Number of times performed each year	Average charge	Average annual income	Potential annual plan payment	Gain or loss

When reimbursement is included as part of a negotiated capitation rate, indicate the gain or loss as the dollar amount of average annual revenue per procedure. This is a critical component of the decision to participate.

Practice Balance Sheet

The establishment of a baseline of salary-related expenses will be helpful in calculating expenses associated with plan participation. Calculation of expenses per visit allows a comparison of per patient expenses with the proposed rates if the plan is capitated. It is also necessary to ensure that the discounted fee for service will cover overhead costs. To negotiate profitable contracts with MCOs, this cost accounting information is needed.

For practices that were affiliated with a managed care plan in the past, incremental expenses associated with participation also may be determined using this analysis.

	Last year	Year before last
Total practice revenue (including revenues for lab and x ray services)		
Total salary and benefits expenses (excluding physician compensation)		
Total office expenses (supplies)		
Total of other overhead expenses (including charged from ancillary vendors paid by the practice)		
Average annual expense per patient visit		
Divide sum of expenses by number of active patients; divide this total by averaging the number of patient visits to derive average annual expense per patient visit		

Accounts Receivable

What are the practice's receivables according to the payor? Plan contracts sometimes specify how long it take to pay doctors for services rendered. This information should be reviewed and compared with the date for other third-party payers with whom the practice participates. Some plans may pay bills after a predetermined time, for example, more than 120 days from the date of service.

Payor	30 days	60 days	90 days	90+ days
Blue Cross/Blue Shield	______	______	______	______
Medicare	______	______	______	______
Medicaid	______	______	______	______
Self-pay	______	______	______	______
Commercial carriers (list several):				
____________	______	______	______	______
____________	______	______	______	______
____________	______	______	______	______
HMOs/PPOs				
____________	______	______	______	______
____________	______	______	______	______
____________	______	______	______	______

Professional Liability

Do the requirements exceed the amounts currently carried? If so, what is the impact on the practice's expenses for meeting liability coverage requirements?

Name of plan	Amount of liability insurance required
____________	____________
____________	____________
____________	____________

CHAPTER 4

Evaluating a Managed Care Contract

As managed care has become more complicated, so have contracts between physicians and managed care plans. It is not uncommon for a practice to contract with a physician administrative organization (PAO), which in turn contracts with a physician hospital organization (PHO), which then contracts with health maintenance organizations (HMOs) or with employers directly. The focus of this chapter, however, will be on a private practice contracting with a managed care organization (MCO) without any further involvement.

Initial contact from an MCO usually comes in the form of a letter of invitation accompanied by an application for membership. Both documents provide some details about the business opportunity. If the practice does not receive a letter but is interested in contracting with an MCO, it can find the plan's name under "Health Insurance" in the Yellow Pages and request an application.

Many questions must be asked before a practice makes the right decision about participation in a managed care system. Unfortunately, every MCO is different in that the forms, pay schedules, financial stability, etc., vary. Thus, negotiations differ. The success of the managed care system affects the success of the practice, and participation should not be entered into lightly.

Although short contracts may be easier to read and seem less threatening, lengthier contracts are often safer. Regardless of the length of the contract, most contracts are drawn with the expectation that they will be negotiated. Although it is difficult to change the discount from fee-for-service, it is almost always possible to get at least some of the clauses changed. Solo practices and small group practices often incorrectly assume they have little bargaining power. Regardless of size, a practice should, during negotiations, pick the most important issues and prioritize them.

One should also be aware that contracts are written to protect the business interests of the managed care plan, often at the expense of physicians' business interests. A properly drawn contract can protect a practice from financial disasters such as overspending by other groups within an HMO. Other pitfalls that can be experienced as a result of not ensuring a contract include year-end bills instead of bonuses (because of failure to read the fine print) and termination without advance notice for a practice depending on that HMO for revenue. The objective should be a fair contract for both parties. If either party does very well under the agreement, thus hindering the other, this will adversely affect the potential for a successful long-term relationship.

Practices may want to obtain a security deposit or a letter of credit (LOC) if their investigational efforts reveal that the MCO may not pay claims in a timely manner or if the practice is likely to accrue significant accounts receivable with the plan. In the former case, the MCO establishes a security account with the provider for an amount based on the estimated value of the claims to be incurred by the HMO during a reasonable period (sixty to ninety days). The practice and the MCO agree to recalculate the amount of the security deposit (quarterly or semiannually) during the term of the contract to ensure that the deposit is neither significantly greater nor smaller than the claims that are likely to be incurred during the designated period. If the provider is forced to terminate the agreement because of unpaid claims, the security agreement allows the provider to use those funds.

A practice can negotiate with an MCO for an irrevocable LOC to be used as security against nonpayment. LOCs are used by HMOs to comply with regulatory requirements pertaining to insolvency protection. The LOC should not expire without reasonable notice from the issuer. Also, the LOC should be unconditional and in no way contingent on reimbursing the issuing bank or on the bank's ability to bring about a lien on security interests. Both a security deposit and an LOC significantly reduce a practice's risk in contracting with an MCO.

The participating physician agreement and supporting documents contain most of the information needed to evaluate a system. These documents usually include a list of covered services, methods of physician compensation, descriptions of utilization review and quality assurance procedures, and a participating physician's manual. Obviously, not only the contract but also all the supporting documentation should be reviewed. The law does not protect people who voluntarily enter into a bad transaction.

The practice should also assess the progression of each managed care contract and continually monitor differences between contracts. A binder notebook retained for each MCO, listing its current requirements and referring physicians with notes, is a must. Ideally, primary care gatekeeper physicians should keep one copy of the notebook at home and one at the hospital in addition to the office copy so that the needed information is always available. In particular, accounts receivable, from the MCO should be monitored. A management reporting system to track experiences with capitation is also necessary to make informed decisions based on past experience. One may also wish to contract a state regulatory body to determine whether complaints have been filed.

Overall Business Considerations

Ownership

Who owns the plan has a significant impact on operations, marketing strategies, and physician relationships. An insurance company-owned system has many advantages over systems not owned by an insurance company. An insurance company's plans most often concentrate on existing clients as the start-up group, with an attempt to maintain market share through an expanded product line. These insurance-based systems (such as an affiliation with Blue Cross/Blue Shield) have the financial resources to weather the inevitable shakeout in markets that will occur with numerous plans all in the start-up phase. Almost all managed care plans lose money during the first two years of operations.

The Plan's Financial and Administrative Structure

Who are the founders, operators, or backers? Are they physicians? Public records on file with the primary regulator of the managed care plan if it is an HMO [certain preferred provider organizations (PPOs) and point-of-sale (POS) plans are also regulated by state laws; see Chapter 5 and Appendix A for further information] are a source for this information as well. All systems should provide this information in the introductory packet of materials.

Other key questions include how the medical director fits into the chain of command. Also, who sits on the board of directors? Who are top managers, and what is their experience?

Name of plan	Owners
____________________	____________________
____________________	____________________
____________________	____________________

Capitalization

A PPO will require about $4 million and an HMO about twice that to carry them through initial marketing and development to reach a financial break-even point.

The Plan's Historical Financial Performance

It is important to determine the financial history of the plan in order to better predict the possibilities for success, and if proper funds exist for marketing paying withholds and timely reimbursements.

Name of plan	Years in business	Is it profit-able?	When is it projected to have a positive cash flow?
________________	_____	Yes No	________________
________________	_____	Yes No	________________
________________	_____	Yes No	________________

Cost Management

The plan must have an effective system for cost management, including data management systems that monitor enrollment, process claims, and handle finance, marketing, and quality assurance. In addition, the system must be able to monitor reimbursement schedules for large providers that allow the plan to charge premiums that are competitive with those of other health plans.

Network

The initial success of a system may be determined by the degree of contact it has with major employer groups in the community. To ensure growth, a managed care system must have an accessible, respected network of physicians and hospitals and be able to obtain comprehensive care from that network comprehensive care from that network.

The Plan's Organizational Structure

Indicate from among the following those factors which apply to the plan:

____ National system affiliation

____ Regional system affiliation

____ Local system plan

____ Hospital-sponsored

____ Group practice-sponsored

____ Insurance company-sponsored

____ Physician network-sponsored

____ Not for profit

If the MCO is part of a national chain, how much autonomy does the local management have?

Use of Name

A practice should retain prior approval authority before allowing its name to be used in marketing a plan. Hospitals that are seeking to align themselves more closely with community physicians/providers are developing physician practice associations to represent physicians' in contractual relationships with managed care plans. Physicians joining plans through any practice association should determine how their names are used in publicity in their role as associates of a particular hospital.

Allocations

What percentage of the patient premium is allocated to patient care, administration, and marketing? What percentage of the premium is earmarked for primary care services or specialist services? What are the actuarial assumptions underlying the reimbursement schedule? On a national basis, managed care plans typically spend

- 30 to 40 percent on hospital care
- 35 to 40 percent on physician care (includes primary and specialty care)
- 13 to 20 percent on advertising
- 2 to 8 percent on catastrophic reserves
- 10 to 25 percent on administration
- 5 to 15 percent for program expansion

Definitions

Practices should read, not gloss over, the definitions. Although the doctor may believe that the definitions of *quality assurance*, *emergency referral*, and *specialist* are self-evident, the definitions used by a managed care plan can adversely affect a practice's reimbursement. The problem in some contracts is that certain key terms, such as *capitation payment*, are not clearly defined. This should be addressed in contract negotiations. Other principal terms include *service area* and *experimental*.

Federal Qualification: Public Law 93–922

In the event of bankruptcy, federal qualification of an HMO (all managed care plans are federally qualified) sometimes assures that the physician will be reimbursed for charges incurred by patients. A marketing advantage is gained here because federal qualification provides employer mandate capability. The Health Care Financing Administration (HCFA) charges a fee to certify HMOs.

Exclusive Contracts

Is the contract exclusive for the physician's practice, the MCO, or both? Can a physician contract with competing systems? Will competing practices also handle patients for the MCO? In most cases, exclusivity is not to the physician's benefit. In mature markets, however, exclusivity can sometimes enhance a practice's growth if the plan has a large membership in the practice's area and is willing to limit the number of plan physicians in the same specialty. What other physcians in the area are members? One should obtain names and phone numbers and contact the other doctors to learn about their experience with the MCO.

Reporting Requirements

The practice should specify which reports it wants from the MCO. Similarly, the MCO should spell out data requirements concerning the care rendered by the practice.

Trial Period

Is there a trial period of, for example, sixty days in which the MCO will allow the practice to cancel the contract if it is not satisfied with the arrangement? Does this go both ways? Can the MCO cancel if it is not happy with the practice?

Provider Manual

Many managed care plans incorporate a provider manual and other exhibits or appendixes into an agreement for reference. Before signing, the practice physicians should review all ancillary materials referenced in the contract. For instance, some contracts state that the physician agrees to abide by the policies, rules, regulations, and procedures of the plan's utilization management or quality assurance program as described in the physician's manual. The doctor must be cognizant of the responsibilities and liabilities mandated by such programs. There may be monetary penalties for not following utilization management policies and procedures or for failure to participate in mandatory peer review committees. Neither of these items may be mentioned in the contract itself.

Term

Will the contract renew yearly without any request on the part of either party to continue the relationship? The current school of thought regarding membership is that a practice should first sign on for only one year so that it can renegotiate if the arrangement does not turn out to be in its best interest.

Automatic renewal is a standard feature of many plans. The automatic renewal clause sometimes includes fee schedule changes without notification to the physician, a clause one should definitely negotiate to have deleted. (If a doctor does agree to a plan with automatic renewal, the doctor should make sure that the practice has the right to renegotiate terms periodically). Such payment modifications may reflect the plan and the physician's overall utilization of services or local inflation figures. Alternatively, the contract may stipulate that the floor rises by the increase in the consumer price index each year, a clause that is less onerous than one in which reimbursement can be changed without prior notice to the provider.

Contracts may vary depending on the date of agreement. Once under contract, physicians lose their negotiating abilities for the specified period and may be at a disadvantage compared with colleagues who sign on later. Practices should take heed and consider requesting data on the reimbursement profiles from the plan and contrasting that information to a practice's own data.

Credential Language

Another pitfall is language obligating a doctor to continue to comply with credentialing requirements "now or hereafter promulgated." If the plan later communicates new protocols, a physician may become ineligible for further participation. Also, if the practice adds another doctor, may he or she automatically join the MCO as well?

Medical Necessity/Emergency

If a clear definition of medical necessity and emergency is not spelled out in the contract, one should negotiate for language that states plainly who will determine these criteria. Some contracts define these terms from a reimbursement perspective rather than from a patient care perspective. The physician's liability may be increased under such definitions.

Access to Medical Records

Participation in some managed care plans and their utilization review procedures can create problems, especially if a practice participates in more than one managed care plan. The practice should determine whether the contract provides a realistic amount of notice to the practice for required access to medical records. If feasible, it is best to arrange for a convenient time during the week when the plan's representatives can review records. The contract should specify that access to medical records will be in compliance with all state and federal confidentiality laws and regulations.

Ancillary Services

Does the contract state from whom laboratory or x-ray services must be obtained? Are the services a practice provides in its facility covered by the fee? Can the practice bill separately for services that are not covered? Is the reimbursement level predetermined by the plan?

As plans develop, they often move from providing medical and surgical acute care to including all ancillary care services. The practice could be required to use designated suppliers for laboratory, home healthcare, physical therapy, and X ray's because the plan has negotiated favorable payment schedules. If a practice has multiple contracts, keeping abreast of which lab, home health agency, etc., to use for which patient will become an administrative nightmare.

Other ancillary services may be affected, including pharmacies, physical therapists, and even hospitals. Will the physician be reimbursed for providing specific services related to such referrals, or is the payment considered to be included in the physician's reimbursement?

Many plans do not reimburse practices separately for services performed in the office, such as lab work, physical therapy, and psychological testing by a clinical psychologist. Others place restrictions on physicians utilizing providers and vendors with whom they have a financial interest. Thus, psychiatrists with in-house counseling services may be unable to bill the plan for those services and are not allowed to bill the patient directly.

Contract vendors of ancillary care, such as laboratories, may cut their services to meet the prices negotiated in the community by the managed care plan. Using these companies may cost a practice extra money.

When contracting providers are inconvenient or lack specific equipment, the cost to the physician in increased time is often prohibitive. The contract may also specify financial penalties for using nonapproved facilities. Penalties are sometimes imposed on the patient instead of the practice; this in turn can lead to lost revenue if the patient leaves the practice.

Covered and Noncovered Services

Does the contract define which treatments are always noncovered? Does the contract state who is liable for the payment of noncovered services and when the patient may be billed if the plan does not pay?

Are there limitations on certain benefits, such as psychiatric benefits? Does the plan offer preventive care such as smoke cessation, stress management, and cancer screening? Are there other supplemental benefits such as eye care and pharmacy discounts (an attractive feature from the patient's viewpoint)? How much do these supplemental benefits cost?

To determine the appropriateness of a capitation schedule, it is important to understand which services are considered standard and which may be billed to the system separately. Some plans are marketing several payment systems and coverage programs. One must make sure that it is specified how the practice can find out whether a patient is covered.

The administrative staff should check copayment arrangements during each encounter when verifying a patient's eligibility. Membership cards are often outdated and do not always indicate correct copayment schedules or state whether an individual is still employed.

Guarantee of Eligibility

Is there an eligibility guarantee? Such clauses prevent a plan from making retroactive deletions beyond 90 or 180 days. An eligibility clause also guarantees that if within that time the doctor treats a listed person who is later determined to be ineligible, the practice can attempt to collect from the patient directly. If it is unsuccessful in collecting, the HMO or other managed care plan will pay the practice a fixed amount for services such as the doctor's private fee. Is prior authorization required for hospital admission and surgeries? Can the office staff deal with the forms, policies, and procedures specific to this plan? these hidden costs must also be considered.

Authorization of Second Opinions

Most plans provide manuals which contain operational information that is to be followed in caring for patients. Second opinion guidelines are most often found in these books rather than in the contract. It is important to know who is qualified to provide a second opinion; for example., is the primary care physician considered the first opinion when referring to a surgeon? Can the surgeon be considered the second opinion?

Medical Extenders and Assistants

Does the contract list restrictions on using medical assistants or extenders in certain procedures? When assistant surgeons are required, are they reimbursed by the contracting physician, under a separate capitation schedule, or on a fee-for-service basis by the plan? For which procedures will the plan pay for a doctor to assist? Can a physician assistant be used as an assistant at surgery and be reimbursed?

In some plans the consulting physician and the assistant surgeon are reimbursed by the attending doctor, who is not allowed to collect from the plan or patient for those services. Under noncapitated arrangements the consulting physician and assistant surgeon may bill the plan as other specialists do. Even if the consulting physician is not under contract, the reimbursement may parallel the plan's fees for such services rather than the physician's usual and customary fee. However, if this is not in the contract, the physician may be able to bill the patient for any remaining balance not paid by the plan.

Referrals

Changes of referrals can negatively affect relationships with colleagues and can be risky for patients and the practice if the network is inadequate. Whose approval is needed to refer outside the network? How is medical necessity determined in this situation? Who is responsible for payment, the patient or the practice?

Physicians

What arrangements for the care of plan members is the practice required to make during temporary absences? The physician should decide whether he or she feels comfortable allowing other plan physicians to cover for the practice; similarly, does the doctor feel comfortable referring to specialists in the plan? One must check the plan's list of participating physicians. Are the practice's normal covering doctors on the list? If not, how are they reimbursed for treating plan enrollees? Does this coverage arrangement require special contractual arrangements between the system and the covering physician?

Most plan's contracts define coverage requirements when the contracting physician is absent. Some plans impose financial penalties when the physician goes outside the referral guidelines. Some plans require the contracting practice to reimburse a noncontracting practitioner who provides coverage for the plan's patients. Other plans seek limited contractual agreements with part-time physicians.

Payment

With a fee-for-service plan, the physician should check the time limit for submitting claims. Here one is looking for a six- to twelve-month period. What billing form will be used? (One should not automatically assume that it is the HCFA-1500 form.) What billing requirements must be met to allow for processing and paying claims? Does the MCO provide ongoing staff training for changing billing requirements? Does the contract provide for payment to physicians within a specified period? What penalty or interest charge will be paid to the practice if payment is delayed? When will the late charge be paid to the practice? Some providers negotiate for language in the contract that specifies that the MCO will reimburse the practice at its private pay fee, not at the discounted fee-for-service rate stipulated in the contract, if payment is not made in the specified period.

On the other hand, if the plan is truly a capitated plan, does it pay at the beginning of the month? Many pay on the fifteenth or thirtieth of the month and can thus hinder a practice's cash flow.

When a plan has problems paying practices on a timely basis, this may indicate inefficient claims processing, insufficient enrollees, or a lack of the required start-up funds. To maintain a positive cash flow, many practices request payment performance data before signing a contract with an MCO. This is obtained from other practices locally or by checking other areas where the plan has an established track record.

If inefficient claims processing is the cause of delayed payment, the physician, group practice, or other enrolled provider may be able to help in getting the plan's administrative process changed.

Who handles the coordination of benefits? The ability to request payment from another insurer for the amount due should be specifically delegated through the managed care contract.

Can the fee schedule be changed without prior notice to or agreement by the practice? Are periodic reviews of charges and changes made in the fee schedule? What are the changes based on? An increasing number of managed care plans are looking at a resource-based relative value scale (RBRVS), using the Medicare RBRVS with a different conversion factor. A physician should beware of language stipulating that a fee schedule can be derived using other value scales that are generally accepted in the community.

Does the plan contract contain a utilization "withhold" clause? A withhold clause gives the plan the right to retain a portion of payments to protect against overutilization of resources. If service is as projected, the practice is paid the money in the withhold funds at a specified time (bonus); if overutilization occurs, the plan retains a percentage or all of the withhold. There are plans that use a shared reserve, in which the plan matches the doctor's withheld amount.

Do specialists' fees come out of the primary care physician's withhold? Is the withhold returned, pending utilization, with interest? Can the withhold percentage be reduced in future years if certain utilization standards are met? What are those standards?

Discounts

A physician should note the plan's discount arrangements and the degree to which they vary from usual, customary, and reasonable (UCR) charges and/or standard charges. It is important to ascertain whether the discount is taken from the physician's charge or from a standardized charge that may be based on local charges (an internal UCR or a UCR obtained from other sources).

If the plan is capitated (a payment that is more common for primary care providers), primary care providers must be aware that they may be required to pay for services rendered by other specialists. The manner in which the capitation amount is expressed should be considered carefully. The practice should insist on payment amounts divided by age and sex. The age/sex breakout is significant, because if the medical group accepts reimbursement expressed as a single per member, per month figure, the medical group assumes the additional actuarial risk that the age and sex of the enrollees in the MCO will match the projections of the MCO. Practices should protect themselves from this risk by insisting on age/sex payments.

In negotiating, a physician should attempt to link the fee discount or capitation rate inversely to patient volume. Also, one should be familiar with the term *shadow pricing*, which occurs when an HMO suggests rates just under the indemnity plan price.

If plan reimbursement is based on capitation rates, how do these rates resemble estimated average annual patient expenses?

Name of plan	Capitation rate ($/patient/year)	Average annual expense per patient
____________	____________	____________
____________	____________	____________

Does the capitation rate for the plan vary depending on the degree of physician risk taken? If so, one must compare capitation rates under the various risk assumptions to the average annual expense per patient.

For plans with a withhold pool, how is the pool structured? Does the practice share the risk?

Name of plan	Percent withheld from gatekeeper	Percent withheld from specialist
____________	____________	____________

In many plans, specialists are reimbursed on a fee-for-service basis, with the fees paid from the withhold pools. Withhold pools should be subject to interest payments. Withhold pools should be subject to interest payments. withhold pools also should have stop-loss insurance to reduce the risk associated with providing catastrophic care.

Capitation Rates

If a capitation rate is used, it is usually developed by estimating the utilization rate for each category of service which will be provided by the practice to the enrollees of the managed care plan (Tables 4–1 through 4–3). Utilization rates are estimates based on the prior history of the HMO as reported to the practice making the decision. This data is typically only provided when the practice makes the request for it.

The total number of enrollees in the MCO plan can be determined by utilizing the data provided, after which the data can be summarized and extrapolated. The following example should be helpful.

Table 4-1 Evaluation and Management Services

CPT code	Description	Number of Services	Regular Fee	Extended	Medicare Allowable	Extended
99205	New pt. Level 5	2	$175	$ 350	105	$ 210
99212	Office visit	27	30	810	23	621
99213	Office visit	156	40	6,240	32	4,992
99214	Office visit	19	80	1,520	54	1,026
99215	Office visit	22	100	2,200	72	1,584
99221	Hosp. admit.	0	—	—	—	—
99222	Hosp. admit.	20	150	3,000	93.94	1,879
99223	Hosp. admit.	24	200	4,800	118.94	2,855
99231	Subseq. hosp.	424	40	16,960	32	13,568
99232	Subseq. hosp.	417	50	20,850	44	18,348
99233	Subseq. hosp.	12	60	720	60	720
99238	Hosp. discharge	67	50	3,350	53.94	3,614
99284	E/R care	6	75	450	60	360
99251	Hosp. consult	12	75	900	43	516
99252	Hosp. consult	150	100	15,000	64	9,600
99253	Hosp. consult	10	125	1,250	83	830
99254	Hosp. consult	31	150	4,650	114	3,534
99255	Hosp. consult	75	175	13,125	150	11,250
99291	Critical care	13	250	3,250	160	2,080
99292	Critical care	16	125	2,000	95	1,520
		1,513		$101,425		$79,107

Current membership in the XYZ MCO is 60,000 for which one extrapolates the necessary data. The number of procedures performed and paid for by XYZ totaled 42. Using the practice's current fee schedule, this would amount to $518,000 for procedures.

Office visits or outpatient services performed were approximately 1,513, and the total dollars summed to $101,425.

Again, utilizing a hypothetical practice fee schedule, this represents $621,345 annually, or $51,778 monthly. Using these numbers, one can calculate a per patient charge on a monthly basis-$0.86296 on a straight nondiscount rate. However, it may not be possible to secure this contact with XYZ without discounting one's services. Therefore, Table 4–4 provides several discount rates that the practice may select.

After reviewing Table 4-4, one would not agree to an amount below $0.44925 per patient, which is the Medicare payment amount.

Based on this data, the practice may first offer XYZ $0.86290 per patient per month based on 60,000 enrollees, which represents a 0 percent discount over the practice's normal fee. Then, if necessary, the practice should negotiate to a floor of $0.51776 per patient. The goal is to stay well above the Medicare RBRVS amounts.

Table 4-2 Major Procedures

CPT code	Description	Number of Services	Regular Fee	Extended	Medicare Allowable	Extended
92982	PTCA	43	$2,500	$107,500	893	$38,399
92984	Corn. Angio.	5	1,250	6,250	260	1,300
93000	ECG	8	50	400	18	144
93010	ECG Report	278	25	6,950	11	3,058
93015	Stress test	11	185	2,035	130	1,430
93018	Interp. stress	60	110	6,600	42	2,520
93024	Drug stress	5	200	1,000	124	620
93227	Holter Monitor	15	130	1,950	45	675
93268	Pt. reg. test	0	—	—	—	—
93307	Echo	382	300	114,600	180	68,760
93312	Trnesoph. echo	6	240	1,440	160	960
93320	Doppler	298	125	37,250	94	28,012
93501	R.H. cath.	11	500	5,500	228	2,508
93503	R.H. cath.	8	500	4,000	168	1,344
93505	Biopsy	25	300	7,500	256	6,400
93544	Inject aorta	4	460	1,840	330	1,320
93545	Inject x ray	4	460	1,840	121	484
93547	Heart cath.	119	1,200	142,800	340	40,460
93549	Heart cath.	30	1,250	37,500	565	16,950
93550	Visuals	3	1,250	3,750	624	1,872
93552	Heart cath.	15	1,600	24,000	522	7,830
93553	Combined	2	1,650	3,300	606	1,212
	TOTALS	1,332		$518,005		$226,258

Specialists should be very careful about a straight capitation per patient plan. The risk is great: Any increase in the number of services per patient or per 1,000 patients will affect the practice's income substantially. If possible, the practice should try to negotiate a "fee-for-service" for services rendered at a discounted rate. It is important to get as much information as possible

TABLE 4-3 Financial Summary: Range of Possible Capitation Rates

	Private pay	Monthly	Medicare	Monthly
Total procedures	$518,000		$235,174	
Total E/M	$103,345		$88,297	
Monthly capitation	$621,345	=51,778	$323,471	=26,995
100% of fee	$0.86296		$0.44925	
51,778/60,000 of enrollees	$0.86 per patient per month		$0.45 per patient	

TABLE 4-4

Number of enrollees	Cost per each member each month	Discount %	Monthly to practice
60,000	$0.86290	0	$51,778
60,000	0.77660	10	46,600
60,000	0.69038	20	41,423
60,000	0.60408	30	36,245
60,000	0.51776	40	31,066
60,000*	$0.44925	48	$26,955

*The Medicare RBRVS payment rate.

and develop a form similar to Figure 4–1 to determine the practice's ability to care for the increased patient load at the fee offered by the plan.

Review of the managed care benchmarks data indicates that not much financial risk is involved in joining the plan. There are no Medicare subscribers, and the members used a limited amount of medical services in the previous year. However, this information should be updated and changed each year as patient care patterns change. Armed with these data, one can make an informed choice about whether to accept the suggested capitated rate or prepare a suggested capitated rate based on the plan's previous utilization patterns.

When a practice is approached by a managed care plan or contacts a plan about enrollment information, many will now request a fee-for-service by treatment modality, rather than CPT codes. This can be determined by comparing the practice's regular fee to the number of times a service was rendered during the last 6 months.

Office services (E/M care): a typical practice patient encounter record for the previous year shows the average charge for all office services provided for new patients ($99.41); for established patients ($50.00); for x-rays ($64.70); and for lab ($14.53). See the following examples to see how these totals were calculated.

CPT Code	Number of times rendered	Fee	Total fee	
99201	100	$ 30	$ 3,000	
99202	200	40	8,000	
99203	400	60	24,000	
99204	400	110	44,000	
99205	600	150	90,000	$169,000/1,700 = 99.41
	1,700		$169,000	$99.41 is the average fee for new patient office visits

CPT code	Number of times rendered	Fee	Total fee	
99211	200	$ 20	$ 4,000	
99212	500	30	15,000	
99213	3,000	50	150,000	
99214	300	70	21,000	
99215	200	100	20,000	$210,000/4,200 = $50.00
	4,200		$210,000	$50.00 is the average fee for established patient office visits

To calculate the average charge for the previous year:

$161,000	+	$210,000	=	$371,000	=	$62.88 is the average fee for all office
1,700	+	4,200	=	5,900		visits during that year.

CPT Code	Number of times rendered	Fee	Total fee	
71010	500	$ 40	$20,000	
71020	1,000	70	70,000	
71030	200	100	20,000	$110,000/1,700 = $64.70
	1,700		$110,000	$64.70 is the average fee for each x-ray service
80019	600	$30	$ 1,800	
80058	100	30	3,000	
80061	150	35	5,250	
81000	700	10	7,000	
85022	1,000	20	20,000	$37,050/2,550 = $14.53
	2,550		$37,050	$14.53 is the average fee for each lab service

Risk Pools and Bonuses

Are there risk pools? This involves withholding part of the capitation payments to doctors. Risk pools also are an issue with an MCO that reimburses a participating primary care physician through a discounted fee-for-service payment vehicle. With the latter system, while the physi-

<table>
<tr><td></td><td colspan="2">Managed Care Benchmarks</td><td></td></tr>
<tr><td>Group Name
Address
City, State, Zip
Phone</td><td colspan="2">The Medical Center, P.C.
1220 Tift Street
Anytown, USA 12345
404-475-1220</td><td></td></tr>
<tr><td>TMC Physicians
7</td><td>TMC Allied Healthcare Professionals
12</td><td>TMC Employees
35</td><td>Group Type
Multispecialty</td></tr>
<tr><td></td><td>Legal Organization
For-profit professional organization</td><td>Reporting period
1/92–12/92</td><td></td></tr>
<tr><td>Percentage of Group's total Revenue Derived from Managed Care</td><td>50% HMO</td><td>0% PPO</td><td>50% Total</td></tr>
<tr><td>Administrator/CEO
Bob Keene</td><td colspan="2">Office Manager
Pam Miller</td><td>Medical Director for Managed Care
Paula Smith, M.D.</td></tr>
<tr><td colspan="2">Plan name(s)</td><td>State Health Plan</td><td>Pru-Care</td></tr>
<tr><td colspan="2">Plan revenue to group during year</td><td>Over $2 million</td><td>$572,076</td></tr>
<tr><td colspan="2">Percent of total group revenue</td><td>40%</td><td>10%</td></tr>
<tr><td colspan="2">Year services began</td><td>1987</td><td>1992</td></tr>
<tr><td colspan="2">Type of reimbursement</td><td>Discounted FFS</td><td>Capitation</td></tr>
<tr><td colspan="2">Population covered by plan</td><td>Commercial Medicare risk contract</td><td>Commercial</td></tr>
<tr><td colspan="2">Number of enrollees at end of reporting period</td><td>4,250</td><td>60,000</td></tr>
<tr><td colspan="2">In-house utilization review</td><td>Yes</td><td>Yes</td></tr>
<tr><td colspan="2">In-house quality assurance program</td><td>Yes</td><td>Yes</td></tr>
<tr><td colspan="2">Ambulatory encounters per 1,000 members per year</td><td>2,610</td><td>33.76</td></tr>
<tr><td colspan="2">Laboratory procedures per 1,000 members per year</td><td>4,026</td><td>222.2</td></tr>
<tr><td colspan="2">Radiology procedures per 1,000 members per year</td><td>601</td><td>71.2</td></tr>
<tr><td colspan="2">Inpatient admissions per 1,000 members per year</td><td>95</td><td>10.6</td></tr>
<tr><td colspan="2">Inpatient days per 1,000 members per year</td><td>398</td><td>150.91</td></tr>
</table>

Figure 4-1 Sample of Data from Plan Administrator

cian may not be paid on a capitation basis, the physician may still be accepting a significant amount of risk through participation in a primary care risk pool into which the capitation amounts are deposited and out of which fee-for-service payments are made to the provider as services are rendered. The primary care provider may be at risk for 100 percent of the gains and losses in the pool that arise from the provision of defined services or for only a portion (e.g., 25 percent) of that risk in a shared risk arrangement with another party or parties. Physicians must understand the MCO's projections of the amount of services provided to determine the possibility of receiving any of the withheld monies at the end of the year. If, for example, the projections indicate an anticipated rate of 400 inpatient days per 2,500 people and the standard for the physician's practice is 100 days per 1,500 people, there is a good chance that the withhold will be returned.

These risk pool funds cover greater than expected expenses for referrals, hospitalization, etc. This is of particular significance if there are large numbers of catastrophic cases or AIDS patients who could increase a managed care plan's hospital expenditures overnight.

The exact method of determining risk pools must be specified; otherwise, the managed care entity will pay only at its discretion and using its rules. One must ensure that the time allotted for the return of the withhold is spelled out. Also, the practice should determine whether the risk pool return is based on the performance of the group's practice alone, that of physicians in the same specialty, or that of physicians in general. Moreover, the practice should ascertain whether the risk pool is affected by hospital costs. The wider the risk pool is spread among providers, the more likely a practice is to be at risk for actions of others beyond its control.

The plan splits any surplus with the doctor as an efficiency "bonus." In judging whether to join a managed care plan, the withhold should be left out of the picture, since the practice may not receive any of it. Even so, the contract should detail how surpluses are calculated and when (annually, quarterly) they are distributed to the physician members. One must make sure that the contract does not obligate the doctor to cover risk pool deficits. If this is not possible, at a minimum, the practice must insist on capping potential contributions at a fixed dollar amount.

Payer Reinsurance

If the managed care plan is small or new or has had less than optimal financial success, one should request that the plan have payer reinsurance that will reimburse the practice after the plan has become insolvent. payer reinsurance is not just a payment issue but a liability issue and should be a provision in a contract even with a managed care plan that has been around for quite some time. It is important to stipulate in the contract that the practice has the authority to request documentation of such insurance at any time and that the reimbursement rate for patient care after plan insolvency reverts to the practice's usual and customary charges.

Federally qualified HMOs are required to carry insurance that guarantees a continuation of benefits to members for all periods for which premiums have been collected, coverage for hospitalized patients, and the conversion to individual policies without evidence of insurability if the plan becomes insolvent. While the number of MCOs that fail is lower today than it used to be, there are MCOs that will go bankrupt, and so payer reinsurance is necessary. With new plans being favored by the government, one should watch for new companies in this market.

Stop-Loss Insurance

A practice should verify that there is a provision in the contract for stop-loss insurance at a fixed amount per subscriber annually. Stop-loss insurance covers medical expenses that exceed a certain amount per patient. A guaranteed minimum rate of return assures that the full risks of high utilization will not be passed on to the practice. A practice must make certain that the stop-loss level is low enough. For a small group, the level should be $3,000 to $5,000. The physician stop-loss insurance should be for professional services only and should not be tied to hospital services. One must pay careful attention to the way *catastrophic* is defined.

The practice must retain careful expense records on each patient to claim the amounts covered by stop-loss insurance. It is also necessary to establish when the stop-loss policy pays off; a period of 120 days beyond the contract's anniversary could cause cash flow problems.

Does the plan's contract provide stop-loss insurance or reinsurance for catastrophic cases? Contracts in which reimbursement is by capitation should have a stop-loss clause for any case in which services exceed a predetermined amount. This insurance should e case-specific rather than restricted to a certain amount per physician.

Overpayments

If the plan overpays the doctor, there should be a provision in the contract stating that the physician must refund the overpayment if it is identified and requested by the plan within a certain number of days specified by the plan. The plan should not charge interest on overpayments.

Favored Nations Clause

This provision mandates that if a practice contracts with other MCOs for a greater discount in the fees charged under the contract, that discount must also be extended to this plan regardless of the negotiated amount in the contract. Certainly, one should negotiate to eliminate such terminology.

Grievances

How are grievances handled? Grievances can arise with regard to utilization management, quality assurance, payment errors or disagreements with peer review decisions, and services authorized by the doctor but not by the plan. What about disputes pertaining to a doctor who, in the best interest of the patient, refers a patient outside the network in an emergency situation?

What are the frequencies of denial and appeal? The plan administrator can answer this question. Are appeals handled locally or by physicians outside the service area? The practice may wish to become part of the appeals process. Most often, the grievance procedures are outlined in the plan's manual rather than in each contract.

The appeal process for patient care concerns (such as length of stay continuances) should be a multi step process with attending physicians talking to colleagues, not solely to a nurse coordinator. In high-quality plans, nurses cannot deny patient care options or treatment modalities.

How Disputes Are Resolved

What is the physician input on the plan's governing board?

Name of plan	Physician input on governing board	If yes, describe the extent

Performance Deficiency

The contract should also contain a clause specifying how the aggrieved party (practice or plan) should notify the other party of any performance deficiency. There should be a specified period of fifteen to thirty days in which the problem is corrected. Only the problem is not rectified in that period can the relationship between the MCO and the practice be terminated.

The performance deficiency provision is crucial. Without it, a managed care plan could terminate for cause an entire practice because of one practice physician who had been in the news for a single malpractice case.

Another issue germane to performance deficiencies is how such disputes will be resolved: by litigation, arbitration, or mediation. A practice should negotiate for language that calls for arbitration or mediation instead of expensive litigation. The contract should address other details about arbitration, such as the selection of an arbitrator and provisions for attorneys' fees.

Liability / Other Insurance Requirements

The plan should have adequate malpractice insurance and other necessary insurance as well. Is the system's professional liability insurance "claims made" or "occurrence" coverage? With the courts beginning to view malpractice cases resulting from rigid or poor utilization review decisions as partly the responsibility of the plan, the practice must reconsider "occurrence" liability coverage.

Hold Harmless Clauses

Does the plan include a "hold harmless" clause in its contracts? Such a clause can shift most contractual liability to the physician if the plan is sued in connection with the doctor's treatment of a plan beneficiary. Restrictions such as prior authorization, utilization limitations, and restraints imposed under the guise of cost containment may affect medical judgment. If a malpractice suit occurs, the physician, under the hold harmless clause, agrees to assume complete responsibility.

Hold harmless clauses are not found in most contracts today. Physicians should refrain from signing a contract that contains such a clause. They should further ensure that there is no subtle language in the contract that achieves the same purpose. For example, a plan may request that the doctor warrant that his or her quality of care will not be affected by restrictions placed on the physician. This is just one illustration of a hidden or implied indemnity clause that may conflict with a physician's professional liability coverage.

In regard to the liability of managed care plans, in 1990 a California court of appeals ruled that third-party payers and utilization reviewers may be held liable to a patient for damages caused by their refusal to pay for necessary treatments. Interestingly, the court indicated that if the patient had the right to appeal the utilization review decision that forced him to leave the hospital and did not do so, he could not have sued for wrongful denial of care. As a result of this case, some managed care plans may include language in their contracts obligating the doctor to inform the patient of his or her appeal rights at the time when the care or treatment request is denied. Such a clause is another indemnity clause in disguise and should be avoided.

A third illustration of an innocuous clause that effectively indemnifies the doctor would be one that states, on the one hand, "You must comply with UR/QA standards," and on the other, "The physician alone is responsible because he or she is making independent decisions about all the care provided."

Does the plan have a hold harmless clause?

Name of plan	Circle one
______________________________	Yes No
______________________________	Yes No
______________________________	Yes No

Most plans have removed hold harmless clauses from their contracts. However, the same intent may remain in language calling for physicians to assume sole responsibility for patient care.

Malpractice Insurance

Does the contract define how much malpractice insurance the physician must carry? Most physicians carry at least as much as if not more than is required by a plan; therefore, the insurance issue should not present a problem. In instances where physicians have decided to practice without insurance, the plan will determine whether to take the additional risk resulting from contracting with such physicians. One must avoid language that gives the MCO plan the discretion to specify carrier or coverage limits.

Quality and Ethical Considerations

Quality and ethical issues must be addressed as well, particularly if one is considering joining a capitated MCO. For example, in a fee-for-service arrangement doctors may provide unnecessary procedures or services because the financial reward is based in part on the work done. In a capitated system, by contrast, the danger exists that the patient will not be given a necessary treatment or preventive service because the group is rewarded for services not rendered. Thus, it is difficult to achieve a balance when a potential conflict exists between quality assurance and controlling utilization.

Patient management issues are further complicated if the doctor not only provides care but also must be aware of and inform patients about noncovered services. Perhaps the best avenue to follow is to view the practice as a patient advocate within the confines of the insurance the patient has purchased. Neither the practice nor the MCO should risk being held liable if decisions about cost containment unreasonably override prudent medical decisions.

Utilization Review

Does the contract require physician participation in peer review activities on a rotating basis? How much time will this entail? Will the doctor be indemnified (not responsible for utilization review decisions that the doctor took part in which could result in the patient filing a suit against the managed care plan) if he or she is not compensated for the peer review activities?

Physicians who participate in peer review activities for medical societies and peer review organizations usually are granted immunity from prosecution resulting from questionable judgment. State law may or may not grant this immunity to physicians participating in peer review for a managed care system; one must make sure that this is clear. Frequently, the purpose of physician rotation on a utilization review (UR) committee is cost containment purposes rather than quality assurance.

What are the utilization review/quality assurance protocols? Is UR done prospectively, concurrently, or retrospectively? Although practices are rarely able to negotiate changes in UR programs, the nature of such programs should be evaluated to make sure that the programs are consistent with the quality of care rendered by the group and do not severely interfere with the standard practice of medicine in the practice.

Does the contract impinge on the physician's ability to practice medicine prudently by making vague references to cost-effective medical and surgical care? The contract, by its very nature, alters the physician-patient relationship. Treatment authorization requirements, UR, and referral restrictions may have an impact on medical decision making. However, the physician's ultimate responsibility to the patient is not altered by an MCO contract.

UR procedures may be spelled out in a physician's manual rather than in the actual contract. Before signing, it is critical that one review the manual to reduce risk of "breach of contract" and liability for malpractice resulting from UR compliance in the face of questionable medical prudence.

Termination

When may a practice terminate a contract? What, if any, advance notice is required.

The conditions for immediate termination of the contract for cause should be listed. Plans typically list issues such as a doctor's failure to meet quality standards. Physicians, by contrast, often cite failure to make capitation payments on time or failure to pay fees within forty-five days of the due day; termination also occurs when the plan files for bankruptcy. Some contracts with MCOs mandate that if the MCO becomes insolvent or if the doctor's contract is terminated, the physician is still responsible for the inpatient care of members until the members are discharged or until care can be appropriately transferred. As a shield from providing "free" care or care at the contracted reimbursement rate if this is a clause in the contract, a practice must establish that reimbursement for provider care after termination is at or close to its private fee schedule. There should also be a contractual provision specifying what the physician will be reimbursed for covered plan services in the event of the MCO's bankruptcy.

Notification to Patients of Termination

Who notifies patients of a practice's termination? Is there a provision for the plan to transfer members before the date of termination rather than afterward? The physician-patient relationship is the sole responsibility of the physician.

Sometimes there is a provision for a joint letter from the MCO and the doctor advising patients that they have the right to stay with the plan and choose another provider within the plan or remain in the care of a physician who is terminating his or her relationship with the plan. Regardless of whether the system officially notifies patients of a termination with the plan, the physician should do so in writing, with a request for the patient to specify where his or her records should be transferred. One never wants to abandon a patient.

With regard to medical records, some contracts specify that the cost of copying medical records will be split fifty-fifty between the plan and the practice. This arrangement is obviously more equitable than one in which the practice bears all the copying costs. If medical records are copied after termination, they should be copied by the practice, not by the MCO representative, to protect their integrity and the practice' interest, as the practice is the official custodian.

Waiting Period Before Termination

The waiting period to terminate the contract should be reasonable. The shorter the waiting period is, the less loss is incurred if the contract is financially detrimental to the practice. Some contracts have 120 or more days as the standard waiting period; 60 or 90 days is preferable. This should be a reasonable amount of time for the plan to arrange for other doctors to assume care and to inform its members. Moreover, one should double-check to make certain that the practice can terminate the contract without cause at any time.

Settling Up After Termination

The contract should spell out how the practice and the plan will settle up after termination of the contract, specifically, the method and time frame. Some contracts call, for example, for an accounting within 180 days of termination and reimbursement by the responsible party within 30 days after that date.

Miscellaneous Clauses

One must watch out for miscellaneous clauses stating that the MCO may change any provision of the contract after thirty days' prior written notice to the participating practice. This ludicrous language could allow the plan to change the types of services the practice is obligated to deliver. Other "boilerplate" language to avoid includes a clause that permits the MCO to assign the contract to a third party; in this situation the practice will not be able to investigate the finances and administration of the third part. Finally, one should avoid legalese that states that the agreement contains the entire agreement of the parties. Such entire agreement clauses mean that any verbal agreement or MCO marketing materials do not become part of the agreement. If there is such language, practices should ensure that verbal promises made by the MCO are put into the contract.

In regard to termination, one must make sure that the physician contract terms are not tied to the patient contract term and thus cannot be terminated until the patient contract is null and void.

Naturally, the overall goal of addressing the previous questions, as well as the performance of the calculations, is to gain some insight into the financial impact and risk a practice assumes in joining a managed care plan. The "exercise" is not nearly as important as protecting the practice and ensuring competitiveness and longevity. the following pages contain a twenty-two point list which should be helpful in keeping this "goal" in mind.

Twenty-Two HMO/PPO Participation Considerations

1. Stay abreast of new or shifting HMOs, PPOs, MCOs, and independent practice associations (IPAs) in the area.
2. Request applications for those which appear to be desirable (e.g., a new manufacturer just opened in town with a particular plan for all its employees).
3. If the practice's application is refused because "that specialty is closed; we don't need any more XYZ," look for a practice "slant" to you. In other words, what uniqueness would the practice bring to the pool of providers (perhaps the group consists exclusively of women practicing OB/GYN, an orthopedist specializing in pediatric spine disorders, etc.)? One can represent a "positive" for the HMO/PPO/MCO/IPA to market. Also, patients or referring doctors can send letters on the physician or practice's behalf, requesting its addition as a provider.
4. When one applies to many HMOs/PPOs/MCOs/IPAs for membership, they will request a list of the practice's fees. It is better to provide them with a list of *codes* and request their typical allowed amount to be conveyed to the practice. In this manner the practice ensures its ability to establish payments to the practice at the highest acceptable level.
5. If the allowables communicated by the organization are low compared to those of other insurers, state so in the return correspondence. Many plans will reconsider and return with a better approved amount.
6. Establish whether there is a grace period for the practice to change its mind if something occurs that would make it difficult for the practice to participate in the program (thirty to ninety days is the most common).
7. Find out whether there is a clause in the participation agreement

requiring that providers be notified in advance of allowable and coverage changes and have the option of getting out if the changes are unacceptable. Otherwise, a practitioner may find himself or herself locked into a plan different from the one originally evaluated and joined.

8. If the managed care organization wants to negotiate a lower allowable with the promise of dividends or bonuses at the year's end or at an other interval, the following inquiries should be made:
   a. How often are bonuses or dividends paid?
   b. How many were issued last year?
   c. To what specialties were those bonuses or dividends paid?
   d. What was the average dollar amount paid?
   e. Are there any criteria the practice must meet to qualify for the bonus or dividend?
   f. Is there a certain waiting period, or are bonuses prorated at time of distribution (after one year of participation the practice becomes eligible for the bonus, etc.)?
9. How many subscribers does the HMO/PPO/MCO/IPA have currently? How many did it have last year?
10. What is the average age of the subscribers?
11. What is the percentage of male versus female subscribers?
12. Is the practice obligated to treat all patients in a given plan once it becomes a participating provider?
13. Can the services of paraprofessionals (physician assistants, nurse practitioners, etc.) be covered and paid as incident to the physician's service? Are there special supervision requirements? Are there special reporting or coding requirements for these extenders? Are the payments lower?
14. Are laboratory and x-ray services separately payable, or are they rolled into the visit?
15. Is it financially? How do the approved amounts compare between plans?
16. Are there any special claims audits or paperwork requirements?
17. What is the deadline of reimbursement to the practice (within thirty days of receipt, etc.)? What happens if the HMO/PPO/MCO/IPA fails to meet this deadline? What is the practice's recourse? Will interest be paid?
18. If the practice is dissatisfied with a coverage issue or payment, what formal grievance procedure is followed?
19. Does the organization follow any special audit procedures on either a routine or a random basis?
20. Does the HMO/PPO/MCO/IPA restrict referrals to other practitioners? If so, what are the criteria?
21. Could the organization discontinue allowing the practice to be a provider, and under what circumstances?
22. How does the practice end its participation?

Sample Physician Services Agreement

The following contract is typical of the agreements offered to physicians selected to be preferred providers. Many of the terms and conditions can be changed if negotitated.

THIS AGREEMENT (the "Agreement") is made and entered into as of the date set forth on the signature page of this Agreement, by and between the physician whose name appears on the signature page of this agreement (the "physician") and the corporation which appears on the signature page of this agreement (the "Corporation").

I. Purpose

WHEREAS, the Corporation has contracted or may contract with affiliated insurance companies and third-party administrators that underwrite or administer health benefit plans and with self-insured health benefit plans to arrange for the services of contracting healthcare providers to the persons insured by or otherwise covered by such insurance companies and benefit plans; and

WHEREAS, the Corporation and the Physician desire to enter into this Agreement for the purpose of providing the services of the Physician to covered person, as defined below, in accordance with the terms and conditions of this Agreement;

NOW, THEREFORE, in consideration of the covenants and mutual agreements set forth below, the parties hereto agree as follows:

II. Definitions

As used in this Agreement and in the Exhibits hereto, the following terms shall have the following meanings:

A. *Benefit plan*: The contract issued by a Payer, the plan document, or any other legally enforceable instrument under which a covered person may be entitled to Covered Services and which is in force with respect to such Covered Person.

B. *Contracted services*: Those Covered Services provided by Physician that are consistent with Physician"s training, licensor, and scope of practice.

C. *Coordination of Benefits ("COB")*: The determination of which of two or more health benefit plans will provide health benefits for a Covered Person as primary or secondary payers.

D. *Copayment*: The charge, as determined by the Benefit Plan, a Covered Person is required to pay at the time Covered Services are provided.

E. *Covered Person*: An individual who is an insured, enrolled participant or enrolled dependent under a Benefit Plan.

F. *Covered services*: Those healthcare services provided to Covered Persons under the terms of the Benefit Plan.

G. *Emergency services*: Those services provided after the sudden onset of a medical condition manifesting itself by acute symptoms of sufficient severity, including severe pain, such that the absence of immediate medical attention reasonably could be expected to result in:
   1. placing the Covered person's health in serious jeopardy;
   2. serious impairment to bodily functions; or
   3. serious dysfunction of any bodily organ or part.

H. *Fee maximum*: The maximum allowable fee payable by the Corporation or Payer for the provision of a given Contracted Service by Physician to a Covered Person as such fee is determined by the Corporation in accordance with Corporation policies and procedures.

I. *Medical director*: The Physician specified by the Corporation as its Medical Director.

J. *Medically necessary*: Medically necessary means the use of services or supplies, or both, as determined by the Corporation's Medical Director, or his designee, that:
   1. are accepted by the healthcare profession as appropriate and effective for the condition being treated;
   2. are based on recognized standards of the healthcare specialty involved;
   3. are not experimental, investigative, or unproven;
   4. are not solely for the convenience of a Covered Person or a healthcare provider; and
   5. do no involve the use of greater resources than are required for adequate medical care.

   The term *Medically Efficient* and other terms may be used by Benefit Plan rather than, or in addition to, the term *Medically Necessary*.

K. *Participating hospital*: A state-licensed hospital that has been designated by the Corporation as a hospital to which a Participating Provider may authorize the admission of Covered Persons for Covered Services; provided, however, that covered Persons may be admitted to any appropriate hospital for the provision of Emergency Services.

L. *Participating provider*: A licensed healthcare professional, including the Physician, a facility, or an entity that has entered into a participation agreement to provide Covered Services to Covered Persons.

M. *Payer*: An insurance company, third-party administrator, or self-insured health benefit plan that is contractually obligated to indemnify or make payment on behalf of Covered Persons with respect to Covered Services and that has contracted directly or indirectly with the Corporation to arrange for the provision of Covered Services to Covered Person.

III. Obligations of the Parties

A. *Provision of health services*: Physician agrees to provide Contracted Services to Covered persons, to the extent indicated on the first page of this Agreement, and to perform such services in the same manner in which Physician provides services to other patients. In providing Contracted Services to Covered Persons, Physician agrees to be bound by and to abide by the terms and conditions set forth in this agreement and all Exhibits hereto. Covered Persons shall not be discriminated against on the basis of race, color, creed, religion, sex, sexual preference, national origin, health status, income, or status as Covered Persons.

B. *Verification of eligibility*: Physician will be provided with a telephone verification service or other alternative method of verification through which Physician may verify whether a person seeking services is a Covered Person.

C. *Compliance with laws and rules*: with respect to Contracted Services provided to Covered Persons, Physician agrees to e bound by and to comply with all applicable laws, rules, and regulations of the State of Georgia and the federal government.

D. *Medical records/financial records*: Physician agrees to prepare and maintain current medical records and documentation relating to the provision of Contracted Services to Covered Persons as may be required by applicable state and federal laws and regulations. Physician agrees to prepare and maintain appropriate and adequate financial records relating to treatment of Covered Persons, including, without limitation, billing and payment information. Subject to any applicable legal restrictions, Physician agrees to allow inspection and duplication by the Corporation, Payer, or their authorized agents of all financial records and all medical records maintained concerning Covered Persons under this Agreement. Such inspection and duplication shall occur upon reasonable notice during regular working hours. The Corporation, Payer, and their agents shall protect the confidentiality of such records in accordance with applicable legal standards. The Physician shall promptly provide the Corporation with a copy of any report that results from an inspection, audit, or investigation of Physician's records or practice by any regulatory authority.

E. *Liability insurance*: During the term of this Agreement, Physician shall maintain professional liability (malpractice) insurance and general liability insurance in the amounts set forth in Exhibit A attached hereto and incorporated herein by this reference. Physician shall provide Corporation with at least thirty (30) days' notice of termination of such coverage. Upon request by Corporation, Physician shall promptly provide evidence of such coverage in a form acceptable to Corporation. Corporation shall maintain insurance of the nature and in the amounts required by state law.

F. *Professional credentials/licensure*: During the term of this Agreement, (1) Physician shall be duly licensed to practice medicine in the State of Georgia, and evidence of such licensure shall be provided to the Corporation; (2) Physician shall maintain full membership on the medical staff (including full admission and clinical privileges) of at least one Participating Hospital; and (3) Physician shall meet the credentialing criteria of Corporation.

G. *Compliance with Corporation programs and policies*: With respect to the provision of Contracted Services to Covered Persons, Physician agrees to cooperate with, participate in, and comply with the utilization management program(s) as set forth in Exhibit B, attached hereto and incorporated herein by this reference, including but not limited to on-site review, quality assurance, and peer review.

H. *Indemnification by Physician*: Physician agrees to indemnify and hold Corporation and Payer and their respective officers, agents, and employees harmless from any and all liability, loss, damage, claim, or expense of any kind, including costs and attorneys' fees, that result from negligent or willful acts or omissions by Physician or his agents or employees in connection with the duties and obligations or Physician under this Agreement.

I. *Indemnification by Corporation*: Corporation agrees to indemnify and hold Physician and his agents and employees harmless from and an all liability, loss, damage, claim, or expense of any kind, including costs and attorneys' fees, that result from negligent or willful acts or omissions by Corporation or its officers, agents, or employees in connection with the duties and obligations of Corporation under this Agreement.

J. *Noninterference with medical care*: Physician shall at all times provide treatment to Covered Persons in a manner consistent with sound medical judgement and practice. nothing herein shall be construed to require Physician to take any action inconsistent with his professional judgement concerning the medical care and treatment to be provided to Covered Persons.

IV. Compensation of Physician

A. *Billing*: With respect to all Contracted Services provided by Physician to Covered Person pursuant to this Agreement, Physician shall bill Corporation of Payer, as applicable, on a form mutually agreed to, at Physician's usual and customary rate that are charged by Physician without regard to whether a particular person has health plan benefits. billing information provided by Physician shall include Covered Person identification information and an itemization of all services and charges provided as Contracted Services hereunder.

B. COB *recoveries*: After Physician has billed Corporation or Payer as provided in Section IV(A) of this Agreement and has collected applicable copayments, coinsurance, and deductibles, Physician shall seek recovery from payers having primary payment responsibility according to the COB rules of the applicable Benefit Plan. In the event that Corporation or Payer is not the initial payer, Corporation or payer shall pay in accordance with Section IV(D) of this Agreement and will take as credits against such payment amounts any payment Physician has received from the initial payer(s). In the event Physician subsequently receives any payment from initial payer(s) after Corporation or Payer has paid for such services, Physician shall promptly pay to Corporation or Payer the amount of the overpayment.

C. *Third-party liability recoveries and subrogation*: As applicable, Physician, Corporation, or Payer shall also seek payment from applicable third-party payers who have payment responsibility other than as health benefit plan payers. Except that Physician agrees to allow Corporation or Payer to acquire and exercise full and exclusive rights of subrogation whenever a third party, other than health benefit plan payer, is liable for payment for services that are provided by Physician for which Corporation or Payer would otherwise by responsible hereunder.

D. *Payment*: In connection with Contracted Services provided by Physician hereunder, Corporation or Payer shall pay to Physician an amount equal to the lesser of Physician's usual and customary charge or the Fee maximum, less all coinsurance, copayments, deductibles, and recoveries described above. Payment shall be remitted to Physician generally within thirty (300 days of the later of (1) receipt of a fully completed, uncontested claim submitted in accordance with the billing procedures of Corporation, or (2) the resolution of all applicable recovery issues. Any portion of such payment die that is not remitted to Physician within such period shall be subject to an interest penalty at the rate of eighteen percent (18%) per annum, with interest accruing from the first calendar day following the end of such period, and with such penalty being payable by Corporation or Payer, as applicable, to Physician. Corporation or Payer shall not make payment in an amount that, when added to the coinsurance, copayments, deductibles, and recoveries described in this Section, exceeds the amount payable under this Agreement. Corporation or Payer shall not be required to make payment under this Agreement pursuant to billings received later than ninety (90) days from the date Contracted Services were provided unless Physician notifies Corporation within such period that a claim for such services has been presented to another payer for payment.

E. *No balance billing*: The combination of applicable copayments, deductibles, coinsurance, third-party recoveries described in this section, and amounts payable hereunder shall constitute payment in full for Contracted Services. Physician may not balance bill or impose any surcharge upon the covered Person or individuals responsible for their care. Nor shall Physician seek payment from Covered Persons or such individuals for later billings denied by Corporation or Payer in accordance with paragraph D of this Section IV.

F. *Limitations regarding payment*: To the extent that Physician's services are compensated by Corporation through payment to a participating Hospital for the professional component of hospital-based Physician services, Physician shall seek payment for such services solely from the Participating Hospital and shall not bill Corporation, payer, or a Covered Person for such services.

G. *Hold harmless provision for utilization review decision*: With respect to compensation for Contracted Services provided by Physician hereunder, Physician agrees that in no event shall Physician bill, charge, seek compensation, remuneration, or reimbursement from, or have any recourse against a Covered Person, persons, or entities other than Corporation of Payer for any benefit penalties that have been applied to such compensation subsequent to utilization review decisions over which such Covered Person has no control, provided that such Covered Person has fulfilled the notification responsibilities for contacting the applicable utilization review entity as such responsibilities are set forth in the Benefit Plan. Except that, this Section shall not apply with respect to Contracted Services provided hereunder if such benefit penalties apply according to the terms of a Benefit Plan of a self-insured Payer.

V. Term, Renewal, and Termination

A. *Term of agreement/renewal*: The initial term of this Agreement shall commence on the date set forth on the signature page of this Agreement and shall terminate upon the expiration of one (1) year thereafter. This Agreement shall be renewed automatically for successive one-year terms on each anniversary of the date hereof, unless ninety (90) days or more prior to any anniversary, one of the parties hereto notifies the other party of its intention not to renew this Agreement.

B. *Termination*

1. *Termination for cause*: Either party to this Agreement shall commence on the date set forth on the signature page of this Agreement and shall terminate upon the expiration of one (1) year thereafter. This Agreement shall re renewed automatically for successive one- (1) year terms on each anniversary of the date hereof, unless ninety (90) days or more prior to any anniversary, one of the parties hereto notifies the other party of its intention not to renew this Agreement.
2. *Termination without cause*: either party to this Agreement may terminate the Agreement at any time and without cause by giving the other parties ninety (90) days' written notice of such termination.

3. *Continuation of care upon termination*: Physician shall continue to provide care pursuant to the terms of this Agreement, including terms of payment rates, to Covered Persons who are in Physician's care at the time of termination of this Agreement until Corporation arranges for the transfer of such Covered Persons to another Physician's care. Physician agrees, at no charge to Corporation, payer, or such covered Person, to transfer copies of such Covered Person's medical records, x-ray or other data when requested to do so in writing by Corporation or such Covered Person.

VI. Miscellaneous

A. *Entire agreement/amendment*: this Agreement and the Schedules, exhibits, and attachments hereto, in addition to Physician's application form to Corporation, which is incorporated herein by this reference, constitute the entire agreement between the parties hereto with respect to the subject matter hereof. This Agreement may not be modified or amended except by a writing executed by both of the parties hereto; provided, however, that Corporation may amend this Agreement upon one hundred twenty (120) days' written notice to Physician.

B. *Assignment*: Corporation shall have the right to assign, delegate, or subcontract any or all of its rights and responsibilities under this Agreement to any affiliate of Corporation. Physician shall not have the right to assign, delegate, or subcontract any of his rights and responsibilities under this Agreement to any person or entity without the Prior written consent of Corporation.

C. *Severability*: If any provision of this Agreement is held to be unenforceable or otherwise contrary to any applicable laws, regulations, or rules, such provision shall have no effect and shall be severable without affecting the validity or enforceability of the remaining provisions of this Agreement.

D. *Relationships of the parties*: The parties to this Agreement intend that this Agreement will create a relationship of independent contractors between them. nothing in this Agreement shall be construed as, or be deemed to create between the parties hereto, a relationship of employer and employee, or principal and agent, or any relationship other than that of independent parties contracting with each other solely for the purpose of carrying out the provisions of this Agreement. the obligations of each party to this Agreement shall inure solely to the benefit of the other party hereto, and no person or entity other than Payer shall be a third-party beneficiary of this Agreement.

E. *Proprietary information*: All information and materials provided by Payer or Corporation (including, without limitation, contracts, fee schedules, the procedures manuals and operations manuals) to Physician shall remain proprietary to Corporation. Physician shall not disclose or permit the disclosure of any of such information or materials or use them except as provided in this Agreement. Neither Corporation, Payer nor Physician may use trademarks, service marks, names, or symbols of the other parties without prior written permission; provided, however, that Physician agrees that Corporation or Payer, as applicable, may use Physician's name, office address, telephone number, specialty, and a factual description of Physician's practice in directories and other promotional materials during the term hereof and for a reasonable period until the reprinting of such directories and materials thereafter.

F. *Enrollment levels*: Corporation does not make any representation or warranty regarding minimum numbers of Covered Persons that will be patients of Physician as a result of this Agreement.

G. *Notices*: Any notice required to be given pursuant to the terms and provisions of this Agreement shall be in writing, postage prepaid, and shall be sent by certified mail, return receipt requested, to the parties at the addresses set forth below their authorized signatures, or at such other address as the parties may designate by written notice. any such notice shall be deemed received upon mailing, as provided above, to such address.

H. *Waiver*: Any waiver of breach of any provision of this Agreement by any of the parties hereto shall not be deemed a waiver of any other breach of the same or a different provision.

I. *Force majeure*: No party to this Agreement shall be deemed to breach its obligations under this Agreement if that party's failure to perform under the terms of the Agreement is due to any act of God, insurrection, riot, war, natural disaster, or similar circumstance.

J. *Governing law*: This Agreement shall be construed and interpreted in accordance with the laws of the State of Georgia.

K. *Headings/gender*: The headings used in this Agreement are provided for ease of reference only and are not intended to substantively alter the meaning of the provisions hereof. the use of masculine pronouns herein is intended to have both masculine and feminine meanings.

L. *Nonexclusivity*: Nothing in this Agreement shall operate to prevent Physician or Corporation from entering into similar agreements with other parties.

IN WITNESS WHEREOF, the parties have duly executed this Agreement.

Effective date of Agreement: ____________________

____

Name of Physician (type or print)

____________________________ ________________

Signature of Physician Initials

Address: ____

Tax I.D. no.: ______________________________________

____

Name of Corporation (type or print)

By: ______________________ Title: __________________

Address: ____

CHAPTER 5

Rules and Regulations Affecting Managed Care Plans

State Regulation of HMOs

Most states have regulations that affect Health Maintenance Organizations (HMOs). For instance, state regulations often include financial solvency requirements or equivalent provisions requiring that an HMO demonstrate that it can meet its obligations. Some state laws governing HMO solvency take various forms, including requirements regarding minimum capitalization, deposits of cash or securities with a state regulatory agency, guarantees by the corporate parent or a financial institutions, stop loss insurance, and insolvency insurance. These statutes often offer little comfort to practices, since most state laws require solvency proof out of concern for HMO enrollees rather than to protect providers. However, some statutes extend protection to participating practices in certain circumstances. For instance, Florida requires an HMO to satisfy financial responsibility requirements by creating a plan for handling insolvency. The strategy must include payments to "unaffiliated providers" for services provided to the HMO's enrollees. Many states have hold harmless requirements that essentially prevent a provider who has contracted with an HMO from pursuing payment for services rendered to the HMO's enrollees directly from those enrollees.

Insolvency Protection

Some states have guaranteed fund legislation which protects a practice to a certain extent against insolvency. Such legislation may not compensate all providers, however. For instance, the Illinois HMO guarantee fund does not cover providers with hold harmless contractual provisions. Another reason why the guarantee fund legislation should not necessarily be relied on is that it may not generate enough funds to allow complete recovery by providers. Also, HMO guarantee funds may reduce the extent of state regulatory reviews of HMO compliance with financial solvency requirements before certification. Thus, practices should carefully consider the terms of existing proposed guaranty fund legislation and should not assume that the fund will solve all the problems created by HMO insolvencies.

Recent cases demonstrate that HMO insolvencies can result in unanticipated litigation. For instance, a ruling involving the insolvency of Maxicare Health Plans, an HMO formerly headquartered in California, established that nationwide HMOs may seek protection under federal bankruptcy laws rather than submitting to state receivership and liquidation proceedings.

Assuming that federal bankruptcy relief is not appropriate or not pursued, providers in states that have not enacted guaranty funds or other adequate protections for providers will have to rely on the outcome of state receivership and liquidation proceedings. Practices will usually be classified as unsecured creditors in such proceedings.

Regulation of PPOs

A few states have regulations for preferred provider organizations (PPOs) and point-of-sale (POS) plans as well. A list of the primary regulators of HMOs (and sometimes PPOs) by state, along with their addresses and phone numbers can be found in Appendix A. It is recommended that one contact the primary regulator before contracting with a managed care organization (MCO) to ensure that complaints have not been lodged against the MCO. MCOs typically investigate a practice before offering a contract; practices should do the same. If there have been complaints lodged with the pertinent state agency (either the state insurance commissioner or the state health department in most cases) that have resulted in an investigation by the agency, the outcome of the investigation is usually a matter of public record and can thus be obtained easily.

Even if complaints have not been lodged against the MCO, it is helpful to contact the appropriate regulatory body because it has annual statements on file that show

- The financial position of an HMO and whether it has improved or faltered. In particular, one should obtain the records of the risk pool's payout.
- The hospital utilization rate.
- The percent of members over age sixty-five.
- Whether the MCO maintains professional liability insurance and has any medical malpractice claims pending against it (see the section on liability in this chapter). If an HMO is deemed liable for medical malpractice, the physician wants to avoid being the deep pocket in the lawsuit.

It is also helpful to know which agency regulates MCOs because the pertinent regulatory body can sometimes serve as a means of recourse if a practice has a problem with the MCO. For example, if a practice was not paid by an HMO within the specified time listed in the contract, it may wish to contact the appropriate regulatory authority. Or a practice could choose to copy the regulatory agency in its letter to the MCO. If this is done, the MCO may rectify the problem more quickly, often before it is necessary for the regulatory agency to intervene.

Other state information generally available to practices regarding HMOs include state licensing applications, state-required quarterly and annual reports, state medical association reports, state hospital association reports, state security filings, government investigatory reports, and private sector industry reports.

In certain states POS plans are regulated by state laws as well.

Modification of State Laws Regarding Managed Care Plans

Many states have recently passed laws that reduce the ability of an HMO to include features such as utilization review, quality assurance, and selective contracting. This legislation has eliminated some of the basic tools used by HMOs to provide cost-effective care. Some states, for example, now require HMOs to accept more pharmacies into their networks.

Utilization Review Legislation

One example of state legislation that restricts an HMO's ability to manage care is comprehensive utilization review (UR) legislation, which was passed in eighteen states in the period 1987–1991 and requires the licensing of individuals or corporate entities that conduct UR. Several states, including Alabama, California, Illinois, Minnesota, Nebraska, Pennsylvania, Rhode Island, and Tennessee, may be considering similar legislation, according to the Group Health Association of America (GHAA). In passing laws that prevent or restrict these fundamental activities, state legislators have created obstacles to successful managed care operations by eliminating the basic tools used by MCOs to provide high-quality, cost-efficient healthcare services, according to the article "The Rising Tide of State Anti-Managed Care Legislation" by Gary Carneal and Erling Hansen, attorneys with the GHAA, published in Medical Interface, in May 1992.

A Georgia law that took effect on July 1, 1991, requires UR firms to be certified by the state insurance commissioner before they can offer their services. Among its provisions, the statute states that if the reviewer questions the medical necessity or appropriateness of the care of a patient, the attending provider must have the opportunity to discuss the case with an identified provider in the same speciality. A Nevada UR law requires registration with the state insurance department of any person who performs UR and the payment of a $250 licensing fee and a $250 annual renewal fee.

Many states also require that HMO personnel making UR decisions apply to and be licensed separately after paying a licensing fee. In other states HMOs have to comply with UR protocols developed by the state to regulate independent UR companies. Also, Texas, Missouri, and Montana have laws requiring that physicians who review an appeal of a denied claim be specialists in the treatment under appeal.

Carneal and Hansen also found that some states have implemented specific UR protocols for HMOs. In 1992 Indiana enacted a UR bill, and approximately twelve other states were considering similar legislation during 1992.

Any Willing Provider Laws

Other states have begun to pass laws, commonly referred to as *any willing provider laws*, that prevent HMOs from selectively contracting with providers. Currently, approximately fifty laws have been enacted in thirty states that could require MCOs to accept nonparticipating providers into their networks (Table 5–1). For instance, nine states have passed legislation requiring that HMOs reimburse enrollees for services rendered by chiropractors.

In contrast to any willing provider legislation, freedom of choice initiatives grant MCO enrollees unbridled discretion to self-refer out of the plan.

Mandated benefit legislation for specialty and so-called nonessential services covering everything from alcoholism to coverage for well child care has been legislated in many states as well. Carneal and Hansen cited statistics from an issue of the Health Benefits Letter showing that almost 1,000 benefits must be offered by health insurance companies among the fifty states. Some states have legislated certain benefits which must be included in any managed care plan under its jurisdiction. These mandates can cover everything from required inpatient treatment for alcoholism to coverage for expensive experimental procedures, according to Carneal and Hansen. In Illinois alone during 1991, HMOs were required to offer at least four new benefits, including coverage for certain infertility and fibrocystic conditions. At least thirty similar bills were under consideration in fourteen states in 1992.

Federal Qualification of HMOs

Approximately 300 of the 1,200 HMOs in this country were federally qualified as of December 31, 1990, as operational. Although lawmakers amended the federal HMO Act in 1988 to allow federally qualified HMOs to offer a POS product as well, HCFA has not published regulations governing POS plans.

If an HMO is federally qualified, these provisions [42 C.F.R., Section 417.107 (a)(1)] require that it have a fiscally sound operation as demonstrated by adequate assets, cash flow, liquidity, operating surpluses, fidelity bonds covering officers and employees entrusted with handling funds, liability and casualty insurance, and a plan for handling insolvency to ensure that patient care will not be disrupted. While one HCFA spokesperson called federal qualification a Good Housekeeping stamp of approval and, as such, an assurance that the HMO is more likely not to go bankrupt, this federal qualification and the state regulations mentioned above do not adequately protect providers from the risk of nonpayment.

While about 300 HMOs were federally qualified as of December 31, 1990, as operational (providing basic and supplemental health services in accordance with applicable sections of the CFR), many more were categorized as transitionally qualified or preoperational. A preoperational qualified HMO is an entity which the secretary of the Department of Health and Human Services (HHS) has determined will, when it becomes operational, be qualified as an HMO. A transitionally qualified HMO is an entity which operates a prepaid health care delivery system and which the secretary has determined meets the requirements of 42 CFR Sec. 142(b). A practice should ascertain whether an HMO is not federally qualified if it is preoperational or transitionally qualified.

There are federal hold harmless requirements for federally qualified HMOs in addition to hold harmless regulations in some states. A federal provision requires, for example, that an HMO ensure that its subscribers will not be liable for fees that it is legally obligated to pay [42 C.F.R. Sec. 417.107(a)(3)]. HMOs may satisfy the requirement through contractual agreements with healthcare providers, insolvency insurance, retention of

Table 5-1 Any Willing Provider Legislation

State	Chiropractor	Podiatrist	Optometrist	Acupuncturist	Psych/Couns.	Pharmacy	Other
Alabama						Ala. Code 27-45-3	Proposal (Personal Physician) SB 662; SB 41x
Arkansas			1993 Ark Acts 1271 (SB) 679			Ark. Stat. Ann. 23-79-143	
California	1991 Cal. Leg. Serv. Ch. 440 (A 904) (public employee retirement syst.)	Proposal A 1568					Proposal S 917
Colorado	1991 Colo. Sess. Laws: H 19-1092 (no fault)				Proposal H 1016	Colo. Rev. Stat. 26-4-110 (Medicaid only)	Proposal H.B. 1150 (vendors of home medical equip.)
Connecticut*	FOC H.B. 5866	FOC H.B.5866				CT Gen. Stat. 38a-471 (1982)	Proposal H.B. 5866 (Medicine, Osteop, Natureopathy)
Delaware	1993 DE Laws 168 (HB 124)						
D.C., Washington	Proposal Bill 10-299	Proposal Bill 10-299	Proposal Bill 10-299	Proposal Bill 10-299	Proposal Bill 10-299	Prop. Bill 10-299	
Florida	Fla. Info. Bulletin 91-015; Proposals H 1763 and S 1548; Fla. Stat. 641.19 (workers' compensation)	Fla. Info. Bulletin 91-015; Proposals H 1763 and S 1548; Fla. Stat. 641.19 (workers' compensation)				1993 FL Laws ch. 129, 77 (SB 1914, 2006, 1784, 406) Creates FL. STAT. ANN. 408.706	
Georgia	GA CODE ANN. 33-20-16	GA CODE ANN. 30-20-16	GA CODE ANN. 33-20-16	GA CODE ANN. 33-20-16	GA CODE ANN. 33-20-16	GA CODE ANN. 33-20-16	(Doctors of Med. DX of dental surgery) GA CODE ANN. 33-20-16
Hawaii							
Idaho						FOC ID CODE 41-1844	
Illinois	1991 Ill. Leg. Serv. 87-560 (comprehensive health plan) See also Public Health Regulations					IL Rev. Stat. ch. 111.5, para. 1407.03# on 12/31/92 Proposal S.B. 927	
Iowa	Iowa Code 514B.1† FOC Proposal SB 220	FOC Proposal SB 220	Iowa Code 514B.1† FOC Proposal SB 220	FOC Proposal SB 220	FOC Proposal SB 220	Iowa Code 514C.5; FOC Proposal SB 220	
Kansas						Proposal SB 84	
Kentucky	Ky. Rev. Stat. Ann. 304.38-196†	Proposal S 167			Proposal S 146		KY. REV. STAT. ANN. 304.38-196† (Physicians & Osteopaths)
Louisiana						LA REV. STAT. ANN 22:1214	
Maryland						MD Insurance CODE ANN. 354	

Massachusetts	Proposal H 439			Proposals H 1302; H 4256; H 4269	Proposals H 893; H 1918; S 646 H 1913	Proposals H 1109 & HB 5221	Proposal SB 614 (clinical labs)
Michigan	Op. Atty. Gen. 1979; No. 5503, P. 223					Proposal SB 592	Proposal SB 592 (Durable Medical Equip.)
Mississippi							
Missouri‡	Mo. Rev. Stat. 376.427	Mo. Rev. Stat. 376.427	Mo. Rev. Stat. 376.427			FOC Proposal HB 163 Mo. Rev. Stat. 376.427	MO. REV. STAT. 376.427 (Physician, Hospital, & Licensed Ambulance Serv.)
Montana	MONT. CODE ANN. 33-22-1704	MONT. CODE ANN 33-22-1704	MONT. CODE ANN. 33-22-1704	MONT. CODE ANN 33-22-1704	MONT. CODE ANN 33-22-1704	MONT. CODE ANN. 33-22-1704	
Nebraska						Proposal Legislat. Bill 744 Restrictions on FOC proposal Legislat. Bill 339	
Nevada	Nev. Rev. Stat. 695C.178† Nev. Rev. Stat. 616.344				Nev. Rev. Stat. 695C.1773	Nev. Rev. Stat. 616.344 (workers' compensation)	Nev. Rev. Stat. 616.344 (Physicians)
New Hampshire						N.H. Rev. Stat. ANN. 420-842(v) FOC Prop. HB 526	
New Jersey	N.J. Rev. Stat. 17:48E-1(i) (Health Serv. Corp.) FOC Proposal SB 1614 Prop. Assem. Bill. 2747 Prop. SB 2172 & 2185	N.J. Rev. Stat. 17:48E-1(i) (Health Serv. Corp.) FOC Prop. SB 1614 Prop. Assem. Bill 2747 Prop. SB 2172 & 2185	FOC Prop. SB 1614 Prop. Assem. Bill 2747 Prop. SB 2172 & 2185	FOC Prop. SB 1614 Prop. Assem. Bill 2747 Prop. SB 2172 & 2185	N.J. Rev. Stat. 17:48E-1(i) (Health Serv. Corp.) FOC Prop. SB 1614 Prop. Assem. Bill 2747 Prop. SB 2172 & 2185	N.J. Rev. Stat. 45:14-331(e) FOC Prop. SB 1614 AWP & FOC Proposal AB 1221 SB 886 AWP Prop. Assem. Bill 2747 Proposal SB 2172 & 2185	Proposal Assem. Bill 2747 (Physicians, Hospitals, & other licensed provid.) Proposal SB 2172 & 2185
New Mexico§	N.M. Stat. Ann. 59A-46-32† Proposal HB 106 Proposal SB 32B	N.M. Stat. Ann. 59A-46-32† Proposal HB 106 Prop. SB 328	N.M. Stat. Ann. 59A-46-32† Proposal HB 106 Prop. SB 328	N.M. Stat. Ann. 59A-46-32† Prop. SB 328	N.M. Stat. Ann. 59A-46-32† Proposal HB 106 AWP LAW N.M. Laws 49 (HB 234) Prop. SB 328	N.M. Stat. Ann. 59A-46-32† Proposal HB 106 Proposal SB 328	Proposal HB 105 (Dentist, Medicine, Surgery, Osteopath) N.M. STAT. ANN 59A-46-32 (Osteopaths
New York	Proposals Assem. Bill 696 SB 1633	Proposals A.B. 696 SB 1633	Proposals Assem. Bill 696 SB 1633		Proposals A.B. 696 SB 1633	Proposals A.B. 696 SB 1633	
North Carolina					N.C. Gen. Stat. 58-67-70 (HMO chemical dependency treatment)	1993 N.C. Sess. Laws 293 (SB 885) (Ameds N.C. Gen. Stat. 58-51-58)	
North Dakota						N.D. Ins. Codo 26.1-36-12.2	
Ohio						Proposal SB 60	Proposal HB 28 (Medicine, Osteopaths Medicine & Surgery)
Oklahoma	Okla. Stat. tit. 63 sec. 2503†; S 838 Prop. HB 1210	Okla. Stat. tit. 63 sec. 2503† 1993 OK Sess. Laws 53 (HB 1322) proposal HB 1210	Okla. Stat. tit. 63 sec. 2503† Proposal HB 1210		Okla. Stat. tit. 63 sec. 2503† 1993 OK Sess. Laws 53 (HB 1322)	Proposal HB 1377	Proposal HB 1210 (Dentistry & Osteopath.)

State	Chiropractor	Podiatrist	Optometrist	Acupuncturist	Psych/Couns.	Pharmacy	Other
Oregon	Proposal House Joint Resolution 32	Proposal House Joint Resol. 32	Proposal House Joint Resol. 32	Proposal House Joint Resolu. 32 Or. Rev. Stat. 743.722 (only if service performed)	Proposal House Joint Resol. 32	Proposal House Joint Resol. 32	
Pennsylvania			Pa. Cons. Stat. tit. 40; S 1560(f)†			Proposals HB 282 SB 505	
Rhode Island		R.I. Gen. Law 27-41-14(6)†			1991 R.I. Sess. 91-361 (H 5761) (mental health nurse)†		
South Carolina		S.C. Code Ann. 38-33-290†	S.C. Code Ann. 38-33-290†			Proposal HB 3631	
South Dakota	1993 S.D. Laws 275 (SB 222) S.D. Codified Laws 34-1-20 (public employee ins.)	1993 S.D. Laws 275 (SB 222)	S.D. Codified Laws 34-1-20 (public employee ins.) 1993 S.D. Laws 275 (SB 222)		1993 S.D. Laws 275 (SB 222)	S.D. Codified Laws Ann. 58-16-38 S.D. Codified Laws Ann. 58-18-37	1993 S.D. Laws 275 (SB 222) (Medicine, Surgery, Anesthesiology, Dentistry & Osteopathy) S.D. Codified Laws Ann. 34-1-20 (Physicians)
Tennessee						Proposal HB 1277 SB 1409	Proposals HB 1479 SB 1365 (Physicians)
Texas	TX Admin. Code tit. 26, 3.3701 et seq.	TX Admin. Code tit. 26, 3.3701 et seq. Proposals SB 343 & SB 344	TX Admin. Code tit. 26, 3.3701 et seq.	TX Admin. Code tit. 26, 3.3701 et seq.	TX Admin. Code tit. 26, 3.3701 et seq.	1991 TX Sess. Law Serv. 242(H2)† TX Admin. Code tit. 26, 3.3701 et seq.	TX Proposals HB 1472 SB 459 (Dentistry)
Vermont						Proposals HB 208 SB 101	
Virginia	Va. Code Ann. 38.2-4221 (Health Serv. Plans); Proposal HB 1260	Va. Code Ann. 38.2-4221 (health Serv. Plans)	Va. Code Ann. 38.2-4221 (Health Serv. Plans)		Va. Code Ann. 38.2-4221 (Health Serv. Plans)	Proposals HB 1515	Proposal HB 1260 (Medical, Surgical, & Major Medical)
Washington	Wash. Rev. Code 48-44.310 (health care services); 1993 WA Laws 492	1993 WA Laws 492 (SB 5304)	1993 WA Laws 492 (SB 5304)	1993 WA Laws 492 (SB 5304)	Wash. Rev. Code 48-46.290 (supplemental health tx) 1993 Wash. Laws 492 (SB 5304)	Proposal SB 5456 1993 Wash. Laws 492 (SB 5304)	
West Virginia	W. Va. Code 3-25A-31†; A878	W. Va. Code 33-25A-31†					
Wisconsin	Wis. Stat. 609.70		Wis. Stat.			Wis. Stat. 628.36	
Wyoming	1993 WY Sess. Laws 55 (SB 22)	1993 WY Sess. Laws 55 (SB 22)	1993 WY Sess. Laws 55 (SB 22)	1993 WY Sess. Laws 55 (SB 22)	1993 WY Sess. Laws 55 (SB 22)	1993 WY Sess. Laws 55 (SB 22)	

*In Connecticut, the department of insurance may have implemented any willing provider requirements for chiropractors, podiatrists, and optometrists.
‡Missouri is considering bill S 673, a general any willing provider proposal.
†Codified under HMO status.
§New Mexico Statutes 59A-46-32 and 59A-46-32.1 only require HMOs to contract with at least one provider for each designated class. (Therefore, these statutes are not "any" willing provider laws per se.)
NOTE: This chart designates only the states that have enacted or are considering any willing provider legislation by specialty type. However, these proposals and laws are usually limited in scope. Typically, any willing provider statutes are restricted to a particular type of health care entity, such as HMOs, or to a particular program, such as workers' compensation.
Source: *Group Health Association of America* Legal Department (December 1993).

adequate financial reserves, and other arrangements acceptable to the secretary of HHS.

Medicare HMOs

In regard to Medicare HMOs, the Social Security Act [Section 1876(g), codified at 42 U.S.C. Sec. 1395mm(g)(6)] provides that a noncontracting provider may receive direct payment from the secretary of HHS if it does not receive "prompt payment" from an HMO for services rendered to the HMO's Medicare enrollees.

In regard to insolvency for Medicare HMOs, although a noncontracting provider may seek payment for services rendered to a Medicare HMO enrollee, contracting providers are not given relief from the risk of nonpayment by the HMO [42 U.S.C. Sec 1395 mm(g)(c)]. Thus, under federal financial solvency provisions, providers are involuntary and potentially uncompensated guarantors of HMO solvency.

Sources of MCO Information at the Federal Level

Sources of information to determine whether an HMO is solid according to federal laws and regulations include: federal HMO qualification applications available through HCFA's HMO Federal Qualification Operations and Oversight Office in Washington, D.C. [(202) 619–3555], federal security filings, and applications for Medicare Tax Equity and Fiscal Responsibility Act (TEFRA) contracts in the case of a Medicare HMO. HCFA also has a coordinated care office that provides direction and leadership for activities related to managed care and coordinated care organizations. This office is responsible for developing, planning, evaluating, and promoting national programs for managed care and coordinated care plans. It can be reached at (202) 619–2070.

Through these sources and the state sources listed earlier in this chapter, the practice can develop an HMO profile regarding the claims payment history, whether contracting physicians are subject to a withholding and the extent to which the withholding is distributed at the year's end, practice's and patterns regarding retroactive denials of claims, increases or decreases in market share and group enrollments, and the size and quality of the provider network.

Model HMO Act

The Model HMO Act developed by the National Association of Insurance Commissioners (NAIC) requires that contracts between an HMO and a participating provider include a provision protecting insureds from liability for sums owed to the provider by the HMO if the HMO fails to pay. With this hold harmless provision, physicians may find that the law renders them the involuntary guarantors of an HMO's agreement with its enrollees.

Guarantee Funds Legislation

The Model Guarantee Fund Act being considered by NAIC would tax HMOs to create a fund for paying claims by providers and other creditors upon an HMO's insolvency. This guarantee fund, if enacted, should not be relied on by providers as an adequate source for paying amounts owed by an insolvent HMO.

Accreditation of Managed Care Plans By Other Organizations

The managed care industry has increased its efforts to police itself through an accreditation system. Several organizations provide accreditation to managed care plans on a voluntary basis. MCOs generally are accredited on the basis of their selection of providers, benefit design, range and access to services, utilization protocols, quality assurance guidelines, and sometimes finances, depending on the accrediting organization. Knowing whether a managed care plan is accredited is helpful to practitioners who are considering joining a plan in that the accreditation process is rigorous; a stamp of approval of a managed care plan through accreditation often signifies that the plan is solid. Worries about whether a plan is a fly-by-night operation should be eliminated with accreditation.

An organization that accredits MCOs is the National Committee for Quality Assurance (NCQA), an independent, nonprofit institution that as of November 1991 had conducted more than 100 reviews, including state-managed reviews in Pennsylvania and Kansas; another 80 reviews are scheduled this year. Major employers that have mandated that MCOs undergo external reviews by NCQA include Xerox and Ameritech. Some employers support NCQA review because NCQA standards serve as a tool for business to use in measuring progress in the delivery of quality healthcare as well as a tool for making prudent decisions about healthcare. The cost of a basic review by NCQA is $22,500 for a review of an HMO with 50,000 or more members. The NCQA is in Washington, D.C. Its phone number is (202)828–4440.

Another accrediting organization is the American Accreditation Program, Inc. (AAPI), which accredits only PPOs, giving them a higher level of legitimacy. The APPI conducted approximately twenty-five reviews in 1992. The accreditation charges for a basic AAPI review is $9,000 to $11,000 plus expenses for PPOs with a minimum of 6,000 members. AAPI is located in Reston, Virginia, and can be reached at (703) 860–5900.

The Joint Commission on the Accreditation of Healthcare Organizations (JCAHO), based in Oak Brook Terrace, Illinois [(708)916–5600], accredits only certain types of HMOs. Its accreditation charges range between $3,750 and $7,800 for a basic review of HMOs with fewer than 100,000 annual patient visits and $11,300 for reviewing HMOs that handle more than 100,000 visits a year.

A smaller accrediting organization is the Utilization Review Accreditation Commission (URAC), in which managed care plans also pay a fee for undergoing review. URAC is based in Washington, D.C., and can be called at (202)296–0120.

The popularity of accreditation is growing quickly. Health plans have caught on to the fact that quality is a marketable feature to insurers and employers. Physicians should have an interest in accreditation as well, since it may be a factor to consider in deciding whether to join an MCO.

Legal Issues Involving Managed Care Plans

If one is considering the development of a PPO, independent practice association (IPA), or HMO, one should first seek legal advice not only for contractual matters but also because of antitrust laws that may have to be taken into consideration. One may need to be familiar with the federal HMO Act. Moreover, state laws regarding HMOs vary. Some states additionally regulate PPOs and POS plans.

Antitrust Issues

The four applicable antitrust acts are as follows:

The Clayton Act: prohibits conduct which creates lessening competition or generates monopolization of all or part of a market.

The Federal Trade Commission Act: prohibits unfair competition or deceptive acts and practices.

The Robinson-Patman Act: prohibits price discrimination between buyers if it lessens competition.

The Sherman Act: prohibits contracts and conspiracies in restraint of trade.

Sometimes physicians want to join a particular managed care plan but learn that the MCO is closed to new providers of their specialty. As healthcare evolves from a cottage industry to integrated healthcare delivery organizations, excluded providers will continue to question anticompetitive tactics. Since most states, with the exception of Georgia (Ga. Code Ann. Section 33–30–25), Arkansas (Ark. Stat. Ann. Section 23–98–109), Illinois (Ill. Ann. Stat. ch. 73, Section 982b), Indiana (Ind. Code Ann. 27–8-11–3c), Louisiana [La. Rev. Stat. Ann. Section 49.2202 (5)(c)], Utah [Utah Code Ann. Section 31A-22–617(7)], and Virginia [Va. Code Ann. Section 38.2–3407(B)], do not have legislation to serve as antitrust guidelines for HMOs and PPOs, these organizations risk violating the Sherman Act when they exclude providers.

For physicians practicing in states in which there are antitrust guidelines, the following information may be helpful:

Arkansas law: Membership on provider panels must be open to all practitioners.

Georgia law: All healthcare providers within a defined service area who satisfy standards set forth by the insurer must be given an opportunity to make application and become preferred providers.

Illinois law: Insurer shall not refuse to contract with any noninstitutional provider who meets the terms and conditions established by an insurer or administrator.

Louisiana law: No licensed provider, other than a hospital, who meets the terms and conditions of a preferred provider contract may be denied the right to preferred provider status.

Utah law: Any healthcare provider who is willing to meet the terms and conditions established by an insurer for designation as preferred healthcare provider shall be eligible to apply for and receive preferred provider status.

Virginia law: No physician, hospital, or nonphysician practitioner willing to meet the terms and conditions of the preferred provider contract shall be excluded.

As a result, HMOs, PPOs, and healthcare providers have become the subjects of antitrust legislation. One such case, *Northwest Medical Laboratories v. Blue Cross and Blue Shield of Oregon*, involved a medical laboratory and a radiology center that claimed that they were victims of an illegal group boycott after the defendant's prepaid health plan, a closed panel HMO, denied them preferred provider status. The Oregon Court of Appeals, using the traditional antitrust analysis that had been applied to other industries for decades, failed to consider the intricacies that exist within the healthcare industry, however, according to an analysis in the American Journal of Law and Medicine (1991, vol. 17 no.3,pp. 271–288). The judge ruled in this case that the facts were unlike the case of *Hassan v. Indiana Practice Associates* (698 F. Supp 679, E.D. Mich 1988), in which an HMO dismissed a group of allergists who overordered laboratory tests.

The Department of Justice recently stated that a health plan with preferred providers that included less than 35 percent of the area's providers probably would not be accused of an antitrust violation for excluding providers.

The Department of Justice noted that a plan must be mindful not only of the total percentage of providers in the geographic market but also of the percentage of providers within a specialty. For example, a plan may accept only 30 percent of the physicians in its area, but the amount of pediatricians accepted as providers may make up 80 percent of the total number of pediatricians in the area. Thus, the excluded pediatricians could claim a group boycott.

Liability Issues

Although managed care has survived the challenge of opposition by organized medicine, unsympathetic state regulators, and overly protective federal administrators, its success has engendered a new level of exposure to tort liability claims. An October 1991 article in Best's Review by Stephen B. Epstein, Mark Lutes, and Lynn Shapiro noted that the more rigorous the cost containment efforts, the more frequent the opportunities for tort liability.

The article further noted that there are two types of potential liability: imputed liability (the MCO's liability is derived from the tortious acts of its agents) and direct liability (results from the actions or inactions of the MCO itself). One case involving imputed liability resulted from an MCO's encouragement or direction of covered persons to obtain services from selected providers. A case of direct liability resulted from an MCO's specification that coverage was available for certain kinds of treatment or lengths of inpatient stay.

The potential liability of an MCO is an issue for a practice that is considering joining the MCO because if the MCO is held liable in a medical malpractice suit, it could become insolvent, thus affecting any participating doctor. This is a different issue from the hold harmless clause issue covered earlier in this book. There may be no hold harmless clause in the practice's contract with the MCO, but the MCO can still be sued.

Breach of Contract Issues

Some attorneys contend that an MCO has direct liability exposure under contract as well as under tort theories. For example, the contract between an employer group and an MCO payor is one on which a claim contesting a denial of coverage might be based. Specifically, the MCO may be held liable on the theory that it agreed to provide or arrange for the denied care, not merely to pay for care. State and federal laws include language suggesting that HMOs provide, not simply arrange for, care. Courts have recognized this distinction between managed care and traditional indemnity insurance since 1939.

An MCO's contract with a payer may be the foundation for a contract claim. For instance, a Missouri appeals court upheld a jury award of $1.5 million against a physician group for failing to provide adequate medical care to an HMO enrollee. The court held that the injured enrollee was a third-party beneficiary to the medical group's agreement and rejected the argument that the group had delegated its obligations to an independent contractor physician.

Also, if an MCO's contracts or marketing materials promise that the quality of care rendered by its participating physicians will be higher than that provided by other doctors, the MCO may be exposed to a breach of warranty claim even when the care rendered does not subject the MCO or the provider to a claim of negligence. The doctor also can be held liable in this case. The impact of this type of commitment also may be detrimental to the participating medical practice in a malpractice context.

Practices should review an MCO's marketing materials aimed at employers and potential insureds to ensure that they do not specify that care of the "highest quality" will be rendered. Physicians should be required to provide medical services only in accordance with standards established by law. It is important to ascertain whether the plan has the right to use a practice's name in marketing its services and, if so, under what conditions.

A number of states allow tort claims against insurance companies for breach of an implied covenant of good faith and fair dealing in benefits contracts. Insurance bad faith theories also are useful to the plaintiff because they allow courts to inquire directly into the process used to reach a coverage decision rather than confine the inquiry to the correctness of the decision itself. For example, a California appeals court held Blue Cross liable for employing a standard of medical necessity that was significantly at variance from the community standards and for failing to investigate the insured's claim properly.

Practices should be aware of these types of liability issues, especially as they relate to the indemnity of the practitioner. Most attorneys who represent physicians recommend that indemnity be mutual. As was mentioned in Chapter 4, in some contracts the physician indemnifies the managed care plan but the plan does not indemnify the physician.

State Regulators Consider a Model HMO Contract

A coalition of state regulators is developing a model contract to use as a basis for evaluating and approving or rejecting agreements between HMOs and their physicians. The National Association of HMO Regulators has stated that the model contract would help protect HMO enrollees, but the GHAA, an HMO trade group, feels that the model would lead to overregulation, increased legal costs, and hassles for physicians. A driving force behind this proposal was the filing for Chapter 11 bankruptcy protection by Maxicare in 1989, leaving many beneficiaries without coverage and many doctors without payments. A current draft of the contract includes the following:

1. A clause requiring HMOs to enter into contracts with "sufficient numbers and types" of physicians
2. A clause requiring a physician to continue to deliver care to HMO members through the period for which premiums have been paid even if an HMO goes out of business, in effect providing free care
3. A provision ensuring that an HMO shall not subject a member to any out-of-pocket expenses beyond the required copayments and deductibles for healthcare given by a nonparticipating physician

The HMO regulators group hopes to work with the GHAA to modify some of the provisions and present the contract for approval to the National Association of Insurance Commissioners by late June 1993. If the model contract is approved by that organization, it may be adopted by state legislatures across the country. Although a phase-in period of eighteen months is expected, this might require contracts currently existing between HMOs and physicians to be evaluated for compliance with the model.

Safe Harbors Relating to HMOs and PPOs

Effective November 5, 1992, two new "safe harbors" were published regarding HMOs and PPOs, and one was amended. The following describes the particulars of each.

Increased Coverage, Reduced Cost-Sharing Amounts, or Reduced Premium Amounts Offered by Health Plans

The first safe harbor covers health plans operating pursuant to a contract or agreement with HCFA or a state healthcare program. The first part of this safe harbor protects HMOs, physician hospital organizations (PHPs), competitive medical plans (CMPs) and other health plans under risk contract; the second part protects HMOs, CMPs, PHPs, health plan purchasing cooperatives (HCPPs), and other health plans paid on a reasonable cost or similar basis.

These health plans may offer incentives to attract beneficiaries to enroll, such as increased benefits; reduce or eliminate the beneficiary's obligation to pay coinsurance and a deductible; or reduce or eliminate the beneficiary's obligation to pay premiums. In some cases these incentives are mandated under the Social Security Act or approved by HCFA. This routine waiver of copayment, deductible, or premiums are not considered to be the same as the routine waiver by other providers for two reasons. First, a health plan's routine waiver is inextricably intertwined with the offering of a package of covered benefits and is not offered for the purchase of an individual item or service. Thus, the routine waiver of cost-sharing amounts is generally not an incentive to use a particular item or service when it is furnished.

Second, although cost-sharing requirements can serve to control utilization, HMOs under contract with HCFA or a state healthcare program have other built-in incentives to control unnecessary utilization and are monitored by that organization, so that the issue of potential overutilization is dealt with adequately.

For health plans under risk contract status, the only standard is that a health plan may not discriminate in the offering of these incentives but must offer the same incentives to all enrollees unless otherwise specifically permitted by HCFA or the state health program.

For HMOs and other health plans paid under a reasonable charge basis, two standards must be met: The same incentives must be offered to all enrollees for all covered services, and the health plan may not claim the cost of these incentives as bad debts or otherwise shift the burden of these incentives onto Medicare, Medicaid, other payers, or individuals.

This new safe harbor does not protect incentives to enrollees offered by health plans that do not have a contractual relationship with HCFA or a state healthcare program.

Price Reductions Offered to Health Plans

The second safe harbor protects the price reductions offered by contract providers pursuant to an agreement to provide services. This provision is divided into three parts, protecting risk-based and cost-reimbursed health plans that have a contract with HCFA or a state health program and other plans that do not have contracts in which additional standards are met. Three prerequisites must be met:

1. The protected remuneration is the contract provider's reduction of its usual charges for the service. This does not cover reductions only to a certain part of the charge (such as coinsurance and deductible) but covers only reductions in the total amounts charged.
2. The terms of the agreement between the parties must be in writing.
3. The agreement must be for the sole purpose of having the provider furnish services covered by the health plan, Medicare, or Medicaid. It does not cover an agreement by the provider to furnish marketing services, preenrollment screening, peer review, or other noncovered services. For the payment for noncovered services to be protected, it must comply with the personal services/management contracts safe harbor published in the *Federal Register*, on July 29, 1991.

The standards for each of the three segments of this safe harbor are as follows:

1. Risk-based HMOs, PHPs, and CMPs must meet the above three requirements. In addition, except as specifically authorized by HCFA or the state program, contract providers may not bill Medicare, Medicaid, or another state program for services furnished under the agreement by the health plan or otherwise shift the burden of the costs.
2. Health plans reimbursed on a reasonable cost basis are protected as long as four standards are met:
    a. The agreement may not be for less than one year.
    b. The agreement must specify in advance the covered items or services the provider will furnish and the methodology for computing payments.
    c. The health plan must fully and accurately report to HCFA or the state healthcare program the amount it has paid the contract provider pursuant to the agreement.

   d. The contract healthcare provider may not claim payment in any form unless specifically authorized or otherwise shift the burden for the costs onto Medicare, Medicaid, other payers, or individuals. Any claim made directly to Medicare or Medicaid constitutes a false claim.
3. The third part of the price reduction safe harbor protects price reductions offered by contract providers to all other health plans when six standards are met:
   a. The term of the price reduction may not be less than one year.
   b. The agreement must specify in advance the covered items or services; which party is to file the claims with Medicare, Medicaid, or another state agency; and the schedule of fees that the contract provider will be paid (i.e., although it does not matter whether the plan or the provider submits the claim, the parties must agree to a set fee schedule).
   c. Unless a fee update is specifically authorized by Medicare or a state program, the fee schedule must remain in effect throughout the term of the agreement.
   d. The party submitting claims may not request payment for amounts in excess of the fee schedule (this does not restrict the provider from charging a higher fee when it negotiates with another plan or bills enrollees directly on a fee-for-service basis).
   e. Full and accurate reporting of costs must be made by the plan or contract provider,
   f. To help assure that false claims are not filed, the party who is not responsible under the agreement for submitting claims is prohibited from doing so.

The July 29th regulations included this safe harbor, provided the following three standards were met:

1. The hospital may not claim the waived amount as bad debt or otherwise shift the cost.
2. The hospital may not discriminate in offering reductions or waivers based on the patient's reason for admission.
3. The reduction or waiver may not result from an agreement between the hospital and a third-party payer. HHS is amending this standard to exempt agreements that are part of a contract between a hospital and a Medicare SELECT insurer. This Medicare SELECT policy must meet all requirements for such a plan; and the waiver of coinsurance or deductible amounts that is provided for under the agreement must be limited to beneficiaries covered by the insurer's Medicare SELECT plan.

Note: this safe harbor does not protect waiver or reduction of Part B copayment or deductibles by Medicare SELECT providers.

CHAPTER 6

Implementing Managed Care Processes

Managed Care During the 1990s

The recession of the early 1990s and the election of 1992 have caused growth in the managed care industry. Investment analysts are high on managed care plans and the companies which administer them because of their continued growth potential.

Now more than ever, employers are looking to control healthcare costs. One estimate of the average cost per employee in a health maintenance organization (HMO) in 1992 was $3,046, versus $3,573 for a traditional health plan, a difference of 15 percent. The gap is expected to widen if managed care continues to hold annual cost increases below the 15 percent current increases for traditional indemnity plans.

Analysts also predict ample room for growth because President Clinton supports managed competition approaches to containing healthcare costs and has said that he will provide incentives for companies to enroll their employees. Although managed care is firmly entrenched in most major metropolitan areas, less than 20 percent of private sector employees nationally are covered by such plans; neither the public sector nor the overseas market has been tapped, but that is likely to change over the next three years.

Keeping Current Patients

Many practices today are receiving requests that a patient's medical chart be transferred to another physician with a note saying something like, "We love you, you delivered my children, took care of my parents, but transfer my chart down the road." Most often this occurs because the patient has become a member of a managed care plan. If this is a problem, one must consider posting a message similar to the one in Figure 6–1 in a prominent place.

TO OUR PATIENTS

During this time of change, we hope medical insurance will soon be available to all at fair rates.

Many employers are shopping wisely and changing insurers to assure lowest costs along with complete, high-quality medical care. We encourage this action, yet we still want to be your source of healthcare services.

If your employer has changed insurance plans, or if changes are expected soon that limit your freedom to select your physicians, please inform us now. We would like the opportunity to contact your employer and register as a participating doctor with your new insurance plan. With your assistance, we trust we can remain your healthcare provider.

Figure 6–1 Notice to Patients

Participation Evaluation

In some communities, managed care plans health maintenance organizations [(HMOs), preferred provider organizations (PPOs), point-of-service plans, and the like] represent 30 to 70 percent of a practice's revenue, and this will increase during the next decade. After an analysis of the practice has been completed and a contract has been signed, it is time to ensure that obligations to patients and the plan are met. One must understand the fee schedule and thecopay from the patient, which may be collected at the time of service or after the plan pays. Figure 6–2 is a self-test that indicates a practice's readiness to deal with managed care plans.

Next, one should deal with the following billing, coding, and strategy issues.

Managed Care—Rate Your Practice	Always	Usually	Sometimes	Seldom	Never
1. Our practice has the staffing necessary to implement an effective system for working with managed care patients and their employers/plan administrators.					
2. We have a written managed care payment policy for staff and patients.					
3. The physician(s) assist the billing/insurance staff with procedural and diagnostic coding and special reports when necessary, as defined by each plan.					
4. We are timely with claims follow-up and inquiry.					
5. The staff stays updated on managed care issues through review of newsletters and managed care contract changes.					
6. We utilize the most current provider information on managed care plans in our state.					
7. We are familiar with the insurance laws in our state and what managed care companies are registered with the State Insurance Commissioner.					
8. We are aware of local trends in medical insurance benefits and the usual and customary payment rules.					
9. We are on the lookout for methods to simplify and/or automate patient accounting and payment functions with each plan.					
10. We consistently provide patient education materials and plan counseling to clarify the patient's payment relationship with the practice.					

Figure 6–2 Self-Test for a Practice

Billing

- Will a representative come to the practice before signing a contract and explain the do's and don'ts of billing, referrals, etc.? For example, a managed care plan may have a specific requirement for completing the HCFA-1500 form, or, a managed care organization may require codes different from the J codes when reporting which drugs have been administered.
- For managed care plans with gatekeepers, non-primary care practices

may need referral slips from a primary care physician. Are referrals for a certain number of visits or a certain period, such as one month? For surgical practices the referral is usually for one specific problem. Once treatment has been completed for that particular problem, the patient may not return to that specialist without another primary care referral for the next problem.

- Is electronic filing an option? If it is not, one should check with other practices participating in the plan to obtain feedback on rejections and data entry errors. Data entry errors should be reviewed with the appropriate contact person.
- What specialties are considered primary care by the managed care plan? For example, some HMOs and PPOs consider cardiology and obstetrics/gynecology to be primary care areas in addition to family practice, internal medicine, and pediatrics. What is the plan's system of classification? Does the plan allow specialties to have a contract both as primary care practitioners and as specialty providers?

Coding

It is necessary to obtain a fee schedule from the managed care organization, including the fees for following adjunct codes, supply codes, and others codes as applicable. If the services listed below are not-covered, can the practice bill the patient, or is this included with other services rendered and not separately billable? If services are billable, must a form be signed in advance of rendering services, notifying the patient that he or she may be responsible (much like the Medicare waiver of liability form)?

For the codes below, refer to a current CPT code book for complete definitions. This list is abbreviated for purposes of this text:

36415 Venipuncture, G0002 Medicare
90782 Act of administering an injection
99000 Handling code
99050 After hours code
99052 After 10 p.m. code
99054 Sundays and holidays code
99058 Office emergency code
99070 Supply code
99361, 99362 Medical team conference
99371–99373 Telephone calls
99381–99397 Preventive visits
99401–99412 Preventive counseling
A4550 Surgical tray
A4560 Pessary
A4570 Slings
A4580 Cast supplies
A4590 Special casting materials

J0110–J9999 Drugs
L4350–Pneumatic ankle control splint and other L codes for soft goods

One must ascertain whether the managed care plan recognizes the 24, 25, 57, 58, 78, and 79 modifiers. In regard to the use of the these modifiers, what is the surgical package definition for the plan? Does the definition include complications related to surgery?
Does the plan accept codes reported with the 21 and 22 modifiers when justified and when appropriately documented with progress notes or an operative report, respectively? Is additional remuneration possible when these modifiers are used?

Strategies

- Some managed care plans, in addition to requiring preauthorization and performing concurrent review in the hospital, "manage" care in the practice by specifying that the doctor may not see more than five patients an hour. It is important to note whether the plan has a similar clause.
- Many managed care plans specify in the contract that they may examine medical records and other data in the practice after giving reasonable notice. One should review the language that spells out what is reasonable notice (three working days, for example).
- How much physician time will be required for peer review to accommodate such reviews in the schedule?

The physician should keep a notebook with pertinent information regarding the managed care plan, such as contact persons and phone numbers, fee schedule changes and updates, services requiring prior authorization, and referral rules. Also, problems such as being put on hold for lengthy periods when calling, busy signals for hours at a time, and incorrect answers to questions should be documented. These types of problems can influence a practice's decision to renew the contract. Table 6–1 presents samples of "facts" that can help guide the staff in plan compliance.

Establishing a Managed Care Data Base

To ensure appropriate reimbursement and assess the impact of managed care decisions on practitioners, it is helpful to establish a practice profile which depicts the types of patients seen, the sources of revenues available, and the types of services and competition for services in particular marketplace. (See Chapter 5 on assessing practice overlap in areas such as evaluating and monitoring data in an ongoing manner.)

1. Patient data
   a. Age
   b. Income level
   c. Insurance sources
2. Sources of revenue to practice from managed care
   a. Large employed groups
   b. Sources by number of patients covered
   c. Sources by dollar amounts covered
3. Service Information
   a. Competitors for provided services
   b. Competitors' fees and policies

Table 6–1 Sample Facts Checksheet

Action	**Who Does**
Who files the claim?	Provider's office.
What can be collected at the time of office visit?	Office visit co-payment, deductible and co-insurance. For specific amounts, call JJJ Group: 1-800-848-4912, ext. 3636.
What cannot be collected from the patient?	Provider agrees not to "balance bill" for any charge over the maximum allowable as listed on the EOB.
Verification of Eligibility/Benefits:	Call: JJJ Group # 1-800-848-4912, ext. 3636.
ID Card:	See back of page.
Pre-certification:	Call: Care Review # 1-800-558-4353
Pre-certification required on all elective admissions.	Emergency Admissions: Notification required within 48 hours of admission.
Submit completed claim forms/ superbills to:	JJJ Group, Inc. Adams Communications Claims 2600 Eagan Woods Drive, # 150 Eagan, MN 55121 All claims must include enrollee's name, Social Security Number, and group number.
For Questions:	Call: JJJ Group # 1-800-848-4912, ext. 3636.
Contact person:	Jane Bellows 1-800-848-4912, ext. 6321

Data on patients and insurers should be maintained by computer, but one should consider the various ways in which the data can be sorted. Information should be regularly updated, either at each visit or on a periodic prescheduled basis.

Practice Policy

Once a practice has elected to join a managed care plan, its own internal policies and procedures must be updated to include the new plan, the date of agreement and any major requirements which are different from normal practice operations. Instructions on how to deal with the plan are needed to guide the staff. The policies also can be used to keep the practice's decisions in line with the practice's overall goals.

Before successfully collecting from patients or managed care companies, a practice must have a *written* collection policy. Most practices have some sort of informal collection policy; however, the informal policy tends to vary from day to day, to be misunderstood by patients, and to be applied inconsistently by staff members and physicians. An effective policy must be

- Written for the staff and patients
- Applied consistently by the physicians and the staff
- Appropriate to the specialty
- Implemented proactively by written policy and patient counseling

The objectives, of course, are multiple:

- Maximize patient support by reducing confusion and misunderstanding
- Maximize cash flow and reduce losses
- Maximize the use of staff time by limiting confusion and questions, thus reducing stress on the staff and physicians
- Improve patient support in the managed care program
- Always have an updated fee schedule which can be reviewed with the patient for copay and deductible

The following topics should be included:

1. A "fair warning" policy.
2. Strict adherence to fees as dictated by each plan.
3. Only the office manager will have the authority to negotiate fees or decide on changing fees for a plan.
4. A schedule for sending final notices and turning patients over to collections (determine what restrictions on this may be listed in the contract).
5. Credit terms and conditions are explained to the staff and the patients.

6. Procedures for formal dismissal of patients for noncompliance with instructions and/or payment, notifying the plan.

A Collection Policy Test

The following questions should be asked about the practice's collection policy.

1. Is it fair to the majority of parties involved?
2. Is it consistently applied?
3. Is it understandable to all parties?
4. Is it flexible?
5. Does it improve the collection rate for the copay and deductible and for noncovered services?

Telephone Information for New Patients

Figure 6–3 lists questions to ask or requests to make of managed care patients when one is making appointments.

Name of Plan	Insured Card #	Copayment Amount	Second Opinion	Precer-tification	Referral Form	Accident Data	Medicare Secondary

Figure 6–3 Telephone Information for New Patients

Educating the Patient

When the staff members take the time and energy to educate managed care patients on the practice's policies, patient loyalty and rapport are increased.

WHY:
- Improve rapport
- Eliminate surprise and/or embarrassment

WHEN:
- On the telephone
- In the welcome letter
- In the practice information brochure
- On the new patient information sheet
- At the reception desk

HOW:
- Verbally

One should emphasize the common good: "Mrs. Jones, we are trying hard to hold down our administrative costs. Won't you please be prepared to make payment for yourcopay and deductible while in the office? In that way, you will be helping us and your managed care plan keep our fees and their premiums as low as possible.

- In writing

Through practice informationbrochures, signs, and other handouts

Established patients should be asked for updated information. A good question to ask is, "Has there been any change in your plan, address, or employment status since your last visit?"

Essential Steps for Expediting Reimbursement

Here are ten ways to expedite reimbursement.

1. Advise new patients when they make a first appointment to bring with them all pertinent information, ID cards, etc. Convey this information to receptionists from other doctors' offices who call to refer patients. Obtain all pertinent information about the plan at the time of the patient's first visit, including
   a. Patient-specific information
   b. Plan-specific information
   c. Provider-specific information
2. In all cases verify the patient's coverage as soon as the staff members have received the pertinent information.
3. Become familiar with the managed care plans most commonly used by the practice's patients, especially the benefits most commonly applica-

ble to the practice and the reimbursement rate schedule. Develop these as simple written references.

4. Organize the patient accounts work area.
5. Gather complete clinical data to process a "clean" claim.
6. Inform the patient in advance if it is determined that the reimbursement rate will not cover the charges in full (for example, elective surgery or noncovered services).
7. Use correct forms, procedures, and coding systems when filing claims.
8. Cultivate helpful contacts in the personnel department of each employer, managed care company, and in-hospital medical records department.
9. File claims promptly and follow up unpaid claims on a regular scheduled basis.
10. When payment is received from a plan, immediately review the explanation of benefits to verify the amount and challenge the amounts which appear to be incorrect.

The following letter could be sent to all employers of the practice's patients as the practice seeks to be included in MCOs that already impact the practice. The letter defines to the employer the advantages of sending the information.

Written verification of benefits should be requested when time permits. The letter in Figure 6–5 indicates the data needed by the MCO to identify the actual contracted benefits.

Letterhead

Date

Personnel Department
XYZ Corporation
Anywhere, USA

Attention: Employee Benefits Representative

Our practice treats as patients a large number of your employees. So that we can expedite the insurance claims process for your employees, we would very much appreciate receiving a benefits booklet outlining your managed care plan and any other helpful information you might have available.

Thank you for your cooperation in this matter.

Sincerely,

Figure 6–4 Letter to Employer Requesting Coverage

MANAGED CARE PLAN

Plan Name: Telephone No.:

Contact:

Patient: Date of Pt. Info.:

Name of Insured: ID Number:

Address: ______________ Group Number: ______________

____

____

Procedure	(Please circle)
1. Is prior authorization require?	Yes No
2. Is a second opinion required?	Yes No
3. Is another secured opinion required if I am selected to do the procedure/surgery?	Yes No
4. Is a gatekeeper referral necessary?	Yes No
5. Major Medical/extended benefits	
a. Deductible amount	$______
b. Has deductible been met?	Yes No
c. Copay amount	$______
6. Total benefits for outpatient services	$______
Total benefits for ambulatory surgicenter	$______
Total benefits for inpatient services	$______
Payment for physician assistant as assistant at surgery	$______
7. Yearly maximum	$______
8. Lifetime maximum	$______
9. Amount used to date	$______

Address for filing claim

______________ Initial

______________ (Practice Employee)

______________ ______________

____

Date

____

Figure 6–5 Telephone Verification of Patient Coverage

LETTERHEAD

TO:

RE: Confirmation of Maternity Benefits

Patient: Insured:

Employer:

Policy Number: Status:

Date of Conception: Estimated Date of Confinement:

Your subscriber has informed us that he or she has purchased a managed care plan from you that provides for maternity benefits. Please provide us with the actual dollar amount of that coverage with your policy so that the necessary arrangements may be made to take care of any balance due.

Please supply us with the following information:

Does the policy provide for maternity care? Yes No

Is this patient covered by the policy? Yes No

Our normal delivery fee is $

Your benefit is $

Our fee for a cesarean section, if required, is $

Your benefit for cesarean section is $

We thank you for your assistance in this matter. Please use the self-addressed envelope to return this form to us.

Sincerely,

Figure 6–5 Verification of Maternity Benefits

Data for Each Managed Care Plan

To complete a cross-reference table and establish a complete reference file, a practice should obtain full information for each managed care plan you encounter. Large employer groups often have more than one insurance option for their employees (traditional indemnity, HMO/PPO, etc.). This information can be obtained from the patient directly or by asking the employer for a copy of all managed care plans in effect.

Proper Follow-Up: How and When

To maximize managed care reimbursement, an effective and timely follow-up procedure for pending claims is essential. Claims must be filed

INSURANCE PLAN DATA

Group Name
(Employer): Group #

Managed Care Plan:

Claim Form Required: Coding System:

Deductible Amount: $ Fiscal Year:

Co-payment amount: $ Maximum Pay: $

Documentation Required (check all that apply):

- ■ Insured I.D. card
- ■ 2nd opinion for Surgery
- ■ Precertification
- ■ Referral Form
- ■ Other: ______

Plan-Specific Information

Total Annual Coverage: $

Assignment/Balance Billing:

Pre-authorization:

How long to submit claim: Average pay time:

Specific Payment Policies (specimen handling, office visits, trays, injections, etc.).

Contact person: Telephone #:

Title: Date completed:

Figure 6–6 Insurance Plan Data

promptly, and an in-office filing system must be set up which allows timely tracking of outstanding claims and claims which have been rejected or incorrectly reimbursed. A good computer system can often track claims according to the individual insurer or managed care plan.

Each patient account and/or outstanding claim should be tracked individually at thirty to forty-five days. Many practices perform this tracking daily for maximum timeliness and to avoid doing it as a cumbersome monthly task.

One staff member should have the responsibility for following up on managed care claims. That individual will become familiar with key plan contracts and learn how to expedite delayed or disputed claims.

An ongoing problem in many practices is the lack of a good system with which to capture hospital data. To ensure that correct data are collected and hospital services are coded properly, consider using the "checkbook" format. For ordering information, call 1–800–334–5724.

A common cause of delay in filing surgical claims is waiting for dictation to be completed. This is not necessary. A process can be established by which each physician carries with him or her to the hospital a card on which the following information is recorded:

- Patient name
- Room number
- Date of procedure
- Name of procedure
- Fee for procedure
- Name of surgeon
- Name of assistant, if any
- Final diagnosis

When the physician returns to the office after surgery, the card or cards should be given to the appropriate person for posting on the patient's account. If there is a reason not to bill the patient until after discharge, the completed record can be held until that time.

The following steps should be taken:

1. *Prepare the insurance form.* To prevent delays in obtaining an individual plan's claim form, it is desirable to use the standard insurance claim form HCFA-1500. This form should be acceptable for all plans. Multiple copy forms are available to save photocopying time and expense.
2. *Submit the original form to the plan.* For claims where coordination of benefits is necessary between two plans, file both claims simultaneously and let the carriers determine their respective financial responsibility.
3. *File an office copy, along with the backup material or source data.* If one uses a computer, retaining a hard copy of the claim is not necessary.
4. *When payment is received, record the date and amount in the patient's account.* Review all explanations of benefits (EOBs) to determine any discrepancies between the amount paid and the amount billed.
5. *Maintain a separate folder for rejected claims and establish a follow-up and appeals policy.*

Using the Charge Ticket for Capitation Billings

Most practices are familiar with the many uses of the superbill (charge ticket, encounter form, routing slip, etc.) in terms of fee-for-service billing, but now there is a completely new use: service documentation to the carrier for patients with capitated plans.

Since patients with capitated plans have no fee-for-service or direct reimbursement through the carrier, it may seem unnecessary to file a claim for reimbursement. However, many capitated contracts require providers to document the individual services and then submit the documents. The contract may specify that the capitation payment is contingent on the receipt of this documentation. More often, however, the contractual requirement is to submit individually coded services on a monthly basis.

The superbill or charge ticket is a perfect mechanism for doing this. It is a document the practice needs for other purposes (such as cash control for copayments), is familiar to everyone, and has all the information required. One can simply take the copies usually prepared for insurance companies, collect them for the whole month for each separate capitation contract, and mail them to the appropriate contractor in a single batch. This saves time gathering information from the practice's computer system and reinforces the need to create and collect superbills for other internal financial control purposes.

Claims Inquiries

Following are some forms and examples of inquiries which may be useful to a practice. The status inquiry form in figure 6–7 is useful if a large number of inquiries are needed and individual letters would be too time consuming. The sample letters in figures 6–8 and 6–9 are useful formats when a specific issue must be detailed.

Common Reasons for Claims Rejection

Here are ten common reasons for rejecting a claim.

1. Contract expired before the date of service
2. Clerical error by the practice or plan
3. Service rendered before the effective date of coverage
4. Identifying information incomplete
5. Maximum benefits have paid for the year or deductible not met
6. Noncovered services
7. Patient not a subscriber
8. Preexisting condition
9. Plan processing error related to coverage issue
10. Clinical documentation inadequate or illegible

STATUS INQUIRY FOR OUTSTANDING CLAIMS

DATE: ________

INQUIRY By: (Physician/Practice Name) ________
Provider Number: ________

We have received neither payment nor acknowledgment on the following claim:

INSURED: ________ ID Numbers: ________
Date submitted: ________ Service Date(s): ________
TOTAL CHARGE: ________ . ________

Please reply below. Thank you.

REPLY

- This claim was paid on ______ in the amount of $ ______ by check number ______.
- Unallowed charges were ________
- $______ was applied to the patient's deductible.
- We are unable to locate this claim. Please submit a duplicate claim.
- Please provide the following information: ________

________ Plan

Representative: ________
Title: ________ Date: ________

Figure 6–7 Status Inquiry for Outstanding Claims

Not all of these reasons for rejection can be corrected by the practice. A thorough verification procedure and/or diligent clerical attention to detail will minimize many of these claim problems.

Reviewing Follow-Up Procedures

There are a number of ways to keep tabs on a practice with respect to follow-up of managed care plans. Some of these methods require management reporting by the staff with review by management. Others require investigation into possibilities not currently in use, such as participation in

LETTERHEAD

Committee on Physician Services

Claim Number:

Patient:

Date of Service:

Type of Service:

Fee:

Amount of Payment:

Date of Payment:

Dear Sirs:

I wish to request a committee review of the above-captioned case. I feel that the "not medically necessary" determination is in error. A copy of the operative report and/or further substantiating information is attached.

After your review of this request, I will expect additional payment or a full explanation of the amount received.

Sincerely,

Attachment(s)

Figure 6–8 Sample Letter to a Managed Care Company Requesting Claim Review

various types of other plans. There is a list of items for review and a schedule.

ITEM	WHAT TO LOOK FOR
On a weekly basis, review the following:	
Problems in adequate and timely provision of physician information for filing and processing claims	Delays in filing or turnaround of claims caused by physician not submitting charges or diagnoses, or submitting incorrect charges or diagnoses
On a monthly basis, review the following:	
Number and dollar amount of claims by plan a. Total b. Paid c. Outstanding	Percentage of monthly charges and receipts represented by managed care plans, itemized by plan; unpaid claims by type

Claim filing status	Number of claims and $ amount not filed for current month; investigate any unusual reasons for delay
Write-offs of discounts required by plan	Receipts versus amounts filed for paid claims; in light of determination, consider practice's "accepting assignment" status and participation policy
On a quarterly or semiannual basis, review the following:	
All managed care plans	Consider benefits and liabilities of joining available additional managed plans, based on success or failure of current plan(s)
PPO	Is the practice in a good position to competitively bid for certain *capitated* plans?

The Plan Also Evaluates the Practice

In addition to the practice's ongoing assessment of participation in a particular plan, many plans regularly review and evaluate providers, auditing medical records to ensure that they meet the plan's standards. The following managed care plan audit guidelines were developed by the National Committee for Quality Assurance's medical record guidelines (NCQA form # 1189N) to review medical records and are used by numerous plans:

1. Do all pages contain patient ID?
2. Is there biographical and personal information?
3. Is the provider identified on each entry?
4. Are all entries dated?
5. Is the record legible?
6. Is there a completed problem list?
7. Are allergies and adverse reactions to medications prominently displayed?
8. Is there an appropriate past medical history in the record?
9. Is there documentation of smoking habits and history of alcohol use or substance abuse?
10. Is there a pertinent history and physical exam?
11. Are lab and other studies ordered as appropriate?
12. Are working diagnoses consistent with findings?
13. Are plans of action and treatment consistent with the diagnosis?
14. Is there a date for a return visit or other follow-up plan for each encounter?
15. Are problems from previous visits addressed?
16. Is there evidence of the appropriate use of consultants?

LETTERHEAD

HMO

Anytown, USA 12345

Dear Mrs. Jones:

I recently received a denial from your office on claim number ________________ for Mrs. A. B. Smith. A review of my contract with your organization indicates that services of this nature should be approved by the HMO.

I attach my progress notes for the services rendered to this individual on this date. I realize that I have seen Mrs. Jones six times during the last ten days; however, each service rendered on those days was necessitated by a specific complaint expressed by Mrs. Jones.

In my examination of the patient, I found that the complaints the patient was presenting were valid.

After your review of this claim, if you still decide that reimbursement is not appropriate, I request that you forward my request to the peer review group for a final determination.

Should further information be required to support my charges, please contact my office.

Sincerely,

Enclosures

Figure 6–9 Sample Appeal Letter to an HMO

17. Is there evidence of continuity and coordination of care between primary and specialty physicians?
18. Do consultant summaries, lab, and imaging study results reflect primary care physician review?
19. Does the care appear to be medically appropriate?
20. Is there a completed immunization record?
21. Are preventive services used appropriately?

Comments (please list appropriate item number for each specific comment)

Marketing a Practice to Managed Care Plans

In some areas managed care plans may state that they are "closed" to physicians with certain specialties. A practice wishing to increase its patient base may nevertheless attempt to "market" to that managed care organization.

Some marketing suggestions are as follows:

- Inform the managed care organization that the doctor has a subspecialty and provide information regarding training in that subspecialty. If a fellowship has been completed, for example, provide documentation.
- Have physicians who are referring doctors and are currently members of the managed care plan contact the organization and recommend that the practice become a participating provider.
- Write a letter to the managed care organization stipulating that the practice will provide services at a lower fee schedule than do other doctors with the same specialty.
- Have current or former patients who think highly of the practice and are insured by the managed care organization contact the organization and request that the practice be offered the opportunity to be a participating provider.

LETTERHEAD

Managed Care Plan
1234 Main Street
Anytown, USA 56789

Dear Sir or Madam:

Most recently several long-term patients who are at my practice have requested that we seek membership in your managed care plan.

I have also become aware that several physicians who refer patients to me for ___(specialty)___ care are now members of ___(name of plan)___, e.g., ___(insert appropriate other physician's names)___. They have asked that I consider joining this managed care plan to be able to provide continuous service to patients located in the Anytown area.

I am the only ___(specialist)___ located in this immediate area and believe that there are sufficient patients who have coverage under your managed care plan to make my joining the organization feasible both for patient care and for the convenience of the patients enrolled in your plan.

I would appreciate receiving from you in the near future a copy of your current fee schedule and an application to become a member of your managed care plan.

Sincerely,

Figure 6–10 Letter to Managed Care Plan Requesting Enrollment Data

- Provide data to the managed care plan showing that the practice's ordering of diagnostic tests is lower than that of peers within the same specialty. If it is a surgical practice, demonstrate to the organization through data that the surgeons in the practice are less likely to operate than are their peers.
- If the practice has contacts in the personnel departments at some of the employers who are insured by the managed care plan, contact them and ask that they make a recommendation to the plan that the practice be given the opportunity to participate.

Contacting an MCO to request membership is best done with convincing justification. This is particularly true when it is known that the MCO is successful in your area. See figure 6–10 for a sample.

When an MCO indicates that physician enrollment is no longer available, it is worth the extra effort to reverse this decision. The letter in figure 6-11 would be even stronger if it included a member patient request.

LETTERHEAD

John Jones
A managed care company

Dear Mr. Jones:

I have enjoyed serving HealthCare Plan's affiliated patients.

I have recently learned, however, that I may not be able to continue to do so. I previously practiced ophthalmology as an employee of Dr. Smith and have since opened my own office in Conyers. Naturally, I wish to continue to treat these patients. However, when I contacted HealthCare Plan and your office, I was told that this was not possible, since I would be viewed as a "new practitioner" and enrollment has been closed since 1989.

Mr. Jones, in light of the fact that I have previously treated these patients and many desire to continue to see me for their eye care, I am respectfully requesting an exception to the "closed" enrollment policy.

Please consider my request carefully, as there are few ophthalmologists in my area to treat patients.

Thanking you in advance, I eagerly await your favorable response.

Sincerely,

Figure 6–11 **Sample Letter to Managed Care Company Requesting Reconsideration of "Closed" Status**

APPENDIX A

Primary Regulators by State

Regulation of HMOs

Many practices are unaware that health maintenance organizations (HMOs) are governed by a specific HMO law in most states (the exception are Hawaii and wisconsin; in Washington, D.C., HMOs are not subject to insurance laws unless they are organized as insurers) and are regulated in Washington, D.C., by the insurance commissioner, the department of health, or the corporation commission.

With the large number of HMOs in many areas, it is helpful to know which state agency governs HMOs so that one can address problems that remain unresolved after several attempts.

In many states two agencies regulate HMOs but only one serves as the primary regulator. The following list of states, laws governing HMOs, primary regulators, and phone numbers should assist practices that have had difficulty with HMOs. The list should also be valuable to practices that wish to contact the appropriate state agency before joining an HMO.

Alabama—HMO Act
Mike Weaver
Commissioner of Insurance
Alabama Dept. of Insurance
135 South Union Street
P.O. Box 303351
Montgomery, AL 36130–3401
(205) 269–3550

Alaska—HMO Act
Paul Roller
Director of Insurance
Division of Insurance
Alaska Dept. of Commerce & Economic Development

Arizona—Health Care Services Organization Law
Susan Gallinger, Director
Arizona Dept. of Insurance
3030 N. Third St. Suite 1100
Phoenix, AZ 85012
(602) 255–5400

Arkansas—HMO Act
Lee douglas
Commissioner of Insurance
Arkansas Dept. of Insurance
1123 S. University
Suite 400
Little Rock, AR 72204–1699

California—Knox-Keene Act
Thomas Sayles
Commissioner, Dept. of Corporations
California Dept. of Corporations
3700 Wilshire Blvd., Suite 600
Los Angeles, CA 90010
(213) 736–3481

Colorado—HMO Act
Joanne Hill
Commissioner of Insurance
Colorado Div. of Insurance
1560 Broadway
Suite 850 Denver CO 80202
(303) 874–7499

Connecticut—Health Care Center Act
Robert R. Googins
Commissioner
Connecticut Insurance Dept.
P.O. Box 816
Hartford, CT 06142–0816
(203) 297–3801

Delaware—HMO Act
Lester Wright, MD
Director, Div. of Public Health & Human Services
P.O. Box 637
Dover, DE 19903
(302) 739–4701

Florida—HMO Law
Tom Gallagher
FL Ins. Commissioner & Treasurer
Dept. of Insurance
State Capitol
Plaza Level Eleven
Tallahassee, FL 32399–0300
(904) 922–3100

Georgia—HMO Law
Tim Ryles
Commissioner of Insurance
7th Floor West Tower
Floyd Memorial Bldg.
2 Martin L. King Jr. Drive
Atlanta, GA 30334
(404) 656–2056

Hawaii—no law currently
Keith Ahue
Director, Depat. of Labor and Industrial Relation
830 Punchbowl Street
Honolulu, HI 96813
(808) 586–8844

Idaho—HMO Law
Anthony Fagiano
Director of Insurance
Idaho Dept. of Insurance

700 W. State Street
Boise, ID 83720
(208) 334–2250

Illinois–HMO Act
Zack Stamp, Director
Illinois Dept. of Insurance
320 W. Washington Street, 4th Floor
Springfield, IL 62767
(217) 782–4515

Indiana–Prepaid Health Care Delivery Plans Law
John F. Mortell
Insurance Commissioner
Indiana Dept. of Insurance
311 W. Washington Street, Suite 300
Indianapolis, IN 46204–2787
(317) 232–2385

Iowa–HMO Law
David Lyons
Commissioner of Insurance
Insurance Dept. of Iowa
Lucas State Office Bldg.
6th Floor
Des Moines, IA 50319
(515) 281–5705

Kansas–HMO Act
Ron Todd
Commissioner
Kansas Dept. of Insurance
State Office Bldg.
420 SW 9th Street
Topeka, KS 66612–1678
(913) 296–3071

Kentucky–HMO Act
Elizabeth Wright
KY Commissioner of Insurance
229 West Main Street
Frankfort, KY 40602
(502) 564–3630

Louisiana–HMO Act
Jim Brown
Insurance Commissioner
Louisiana Dept. of Insurance
950 N. 5th Street
Baton Rouge, LA 70804–9214
(504) 343–5900

Maine–HMO Act
Jeri Brown
Acting superintendent of Insurance
Maine Bureau of Insurance
State House, Station 34
Augusta, ME 04333
(207) 582–8707

Maryland–HMO Act
John A. Donaho
Insurance Commissioner
Dept. of Licensing & Regulation
Stanbalt Bldg., 7th Fl. South
501 St. Paul Place
Baltimore, MD 21207
(410) 333–2520

Massachusetts–HMO Law
Susan K. Scott
Acting Commissioner of Insurance
Division of Insurance
Exec. Office of Consumer Affairs
280 Friend St.
Boston, Ma. 02114
(617) 727–7189, ext. 515

Michigan–HMO Law
David Dykhous
Commissioner
Insurance Bureau
Michigan Dept of Licensing & Regulation
611 W. Ottawa Street, 2nd Fl. North
Lansing, MI 48909
(517) 373–9273

Minnesota–HMO Act
Marlene E. Marschall
Minnesota Dept. of Health
717 Delaware Street, SE
Minneapolis, MN 55440
(612) 623–5460

Mississippi–HMO Act
Alton B. Cobb, MD
Executive Offices & Secretary
Mississippi Dept. of Health
2423 N. State Street
Jackson, MS 39215–1700
(601) 960–7635

Missouri–HMO Law Lewis E. Malahn
Director, Div. of Insurance
Missouri Dept. of Insurance
P.O. Box 690
Jefferson City, MO 65102–0690
(314) 751–4126

Montana–HMO Act
Andrea H. Bennett
Commissioner of Insurcne
Montana Dept. of Insurance
Mitchell Bldg., Room 270
126 N. Sanders
Helena, MT 59620

Nebraska–HMO Act
William H. McCarney
Director
Nebraska Dept. of Insurance
941 O Street, Suite 400
Lincoln, NE 68508
(408) 471–2201

Nevada–HMO Law
David Gates
Commissioner of Insurance
Insurance Division
Nevada Dept. of Commerce
Nye Bldg., Room 312
201 S. Fall Street
Carson City, NV 89710
(702) 885–4270

New Hampshire–HMO Law
Louis E. Bergeron
Commissioner
NH Dept. of Insurance
169 Manchester Street
Concord, NH 03301
(603) 271–2261

New Jersey–HMO Act
Frances Dunston, MD
Commissioner of Health
New Jersey Dept. of Health
Health & Agriculture Bldg., Room 805
CN-360
Trenton, NJ 08625
(609) 292–7837

New Mexico–HMO Act
Fabian Chavez
Superintendent
Dept. of Insurance
NM Corporation Commission
P.O. Box Drawer 1269
Santa Fe, NM 87501
(505) 827–4500

New York–HMO Law
Mark Chassin
Commissioner
NY State Dept. of Health
Empire State Plaza
Corning Tower Bldg.
Albany, NY 12237
(518) 474–2011

North Carolina–HMO Law
James E. Long
Commissioner of Insurance
NC Dept. of Insurance
Dobbs Bldg.
P.O. Box 26387
Raleigh, NC 27611
(919) 733–7349

North Dakota–HMO Law
Earl R. Pomeroy
Commissioner of Insurance
ND Dept. of Insurance
Capitol Bldg., 5th Fl.
600 E. Blvd/ Ave.
Bismark, ND 58505–0320
(701) 224–2440

Ohio–HMO Law
Harold Duryee
Director of Insurance
Ohio Dept. of Insurance
2100 Stella Court
Columbus, OH 43266–0566
(614) 644–2658

Oklahoma –HMO Law
John K Levitt. MD, Commissioner
Oklahoma State Dept of Health
1000 NE 10th Street
Oklahoma City, OK 73117
(405) 271–5161

Oregon –Health Care Service Contractors
Gark Weeks, Director
Oregon Dept. of Insurance
440 Labor & Industry Bldg.
Salem, OR 973310
(503) 378–4271

Pennsylvania–HMO Act
Constance B. Foster
Insurance Commissioner
PA Dept. of Insurance
1326 Strawberry Square
Harrisburg, PA 17120
(717) 787–5173

Rhode Island–HMO Act
Charles Kwolek
Superintendent of Insurance
RI Dept. of Insurance
233 Rishmond St., 2nd Fl.
Providence, RI 02903–4233
(401) 277–2223

South Carolina–HMO Act
John G. Richards, V
Chief Insurance Commissioner
SC Dept. of Insurance
1612 Marion Street
P.O. Box 100105
Columbia, SC 29202–3105
(803) 737–6117

South Dakota–HMO Law
Mary Jane Cleary
Director of Insurance
SD Div. of Insurance
500 E. Capitol
Pierre, SD 57501
(605) 773–3563

Tennessee–HMO Act
Elaine A. McReynolds
Commissioner
Tennessee Dept of Commerce & Insurance
Volunteer Plaza
500 James Robertson Pkwy.
Nashville, TN 37219

Texas–HMO Law
Georgia D. Flint
Commissioner of Insurance
Texas Department of Insurance
PO Box 149104
Austin, TX 78714–9104
(512) 463–6464

Utah –HMO Act
Harold C. Yancey
UT Commissioner of Insurance
P.O. Box 45803
Salt Lake City, UT 84145
(801) 530–6400

Vermont–HMO Act
Jeffrey P. Johnson, Commissioner
Vermont Dept. of Banking, Insurance & Securities
120 State St., State Office Bldg.
Montpelier, VT 05602
(802) 828–3301

Virginia—HMO Act
Steven T. Foster
Commissioner of Insurance
Bureau of Insurance
VA State Corporation Commsiion
P.O. Box 1157
Richmond, VA 23209
(804) 786–3741

Washington—HMO Act
Richard G. Marquardt
Insurance Commissioner
P.O. Box 40255
Olympia, WA 98504–0255
(206) 753–7301

Washington, D.C.—HMOs are not subject to insurance laws unless organized as insurers. For purposes of increasing rates, the superintendent of insurance is the regulator.
Marguite C. Stokes
Superintendent of Insurance
613 G. Street, NW 6th Fl.
Washington, DC 20001

West Virginia —HMO Act
Hanley Clark
Commissioner of Insurance
West VA Dept. of Insurance
2019 Washington Street. E
Charleston, WV 25305
(304) 348–3394

Wisconsin—No specific HMO Law, Service Insurance Corp. Law governs HMOs inpart.
Richard D. Haase, Commissioner
P.O. Box 7873
Madison, WI 53707–7873
(608) 266–0102

Wyoming—HMO Act
Ken Erickson
Insurance Commissioner
Wyoming Dept. of Insurance
Herschler Bldg.
122 W. 25th Street
Cheyenne, WY 82002
(307) 777–7401

APPENDIX B

Glossary of Terms

The patient:

Beneficiary	Employee
Recipient	Subscriber
Policyholder	Insured
Dependent	Member
Claimant	Enrollee

The doctor:

Provider	Supplier
Care giver	Gatekeeper
Specialist	

The explanation of Medicare benefits:

Voucher
Remittance Advice

Explanation of benefits (other insurers)

Carrier	Insurer
Plan	Agency
Fund	Intermediary (fiscal)
Organization	

The insurance policy:

Plan	Program
Policy	Benefits
Contract	Certificate

Actual charge: the charge submitted by a physician or supplier for a service rendered by that physician.

Ambulatory Surgery Center (ASC): a center for surgery of an uncomplicated nature that has traditionally been done on an inpatient basis. ASCs are hospital-based (or hospital-sponsored) or independently owned (or sponsored). One of the advantages of these centers is that they are not yet covered by the DRG system; therefore, hospitals may have an incentive to treat as many patients as medically feasible in a setting where it may still be reimbursed on a cost basis.

Benefit period: carrier-specified effective dates of coverage; can be a designated six-month period, a calendar year, or a plan's anniversary date.

Capitation: the amount of money required per person to provide covered services for a specific period. Capitation is usually expressed on a per member, per month basis. Under a capitated arrangement, the provider (physician or hospital) is paid a predetermined fixed amount per member per month.

Coinsurance/copayment: the amount of the carrier allowable designated to be paid by the patient (e.g., 20 percent coinsurance and 80 percent insurance payment). The copayment can also be a flat per visit amount designated as the copayment (e.g., $5 per encounter).

Competitive Medical Plan (CMP): a legal entity organized under state law which delivers prepaid health care and is similar in many respects to an HMO. A CMPs defined medical package must include physician, laboratory, x-ray, emergency, preventive, inpatient hospital, and out-of-area services. CMPs may also impose deductibles on beneficiaries and set more competitive rates for premiums than yHMOs do. CMPs originated as a result of Section 114 of the Tax Equity and Fiscal Responsibility Act of 1982. The rules for implementing Section 114 were not released until January 1985. Under those rules, CMPs are able to contract with Medicare to serve Medicare beneficiaries.

Coordination Of Benefits (COB): a procedure implemented by the group health insurance industry to ensure that each responsible insurer pays its portion of claims and prevent double recovery of claims by insureds. This allows carriers to coordinate benefits lo limit payments or the costs of services to no more than 100 percent of the actual charges and designate the order in which the multiple carriers are to pay benefits.

CPT-4 (*Physicians' Current Procedural Terminology*): a book produced by the American Medical Association listing descriptive terms and codes for reporting medical services and procedures.

Deductible: the portion of allowable charges for covered services each benefit year for which a patient is responsible before benefits begin.

Diagnosis Related Group (DRG): the payment mechanism for Medicare Part A (hospital).

Downcoding: a change of codes by a carrier on a submitted claim to a lower level of service or a lesser procedure.

Durable Medical Equipment (DME): medical equipment such as wheelchairs, crutches, and canes.

Evaluation and Management (E&M): a term used in CPT, referring to codes for patient visits, hospital admission and discharge, and critical care and consultation services.

Federally Qualified HMOs (FQHMOs): staff, group, and IPA model HMOs that are eligible for federal qualification under the federal HMO law, P.L. 93–222, enacted in 1973. Network model HMOs are usually not eligible for qualification. Several strict requirements must be met for an HMO to be federally qualified. The advantage of qualification is that the HMO is eligible for selection by a company with more than twenty-five employees as one of the two kinds of HMOs the company is required to offer to its employees, i.e., one IPA and one group or staff model HMO. This is known as the "dual choice mandate" of the HMO law. The HMO must make a formal request to the company, and the employees' union must agree to the selection of the HMO. In a federally qualified model, at least 35 percent or the group's activity must be devoted to the delivery of care to HMO members. Another advantage of qualification is that the HMO is eligible to contract with Medicare to be reimbursed on a per capita basis for an amount equal to 95 percent of its estimated cost for total health care services to that person during the year.

Fragmentation: a term that describes coding which utilizes two or more codes when, according to the descriptors, one code would completely describe the procedure. This type of coding error often causes overpayment.

Free standing urgent care center/episodic acute care center: what is commonly called a freestanding urgent care center may also be called an episodic acute care center, since "urgent care" visits constitute only about 20 percent of such a facility's total patient visits. In addition, many states have enacted regulations regarding special staffing and equipment requirements for free-standing centers that treat emergencies. These centers generally provide episodic care for routine or minor emergency problems such as sore throats, sprains, and minor lacerations. They are open twelve to sixteen hours a day, usually seven days a week, tend to be conveniently located, and are staffed by physicians and a small support staff, depending on the size of the facility and its average patient load. Other names for these centers include emergency care centers, immediate care centers, convenience clinics, and ambulatory care centers.

Group model HMO: a system in which physicians are members of a partnership or a service corporation which contracts with an HMO to provide services to members for a predetermined per member, per month amount called a capitation. From this capitation fund, the physicians' group pays its own members according to a prearranged schedule (such as salary plus incentives). Physicians see mostly HMO patients and, as in the staff model, share equipment, records, and personnel.

HCFA–1500: the universal insurance claim form used by physicians and suppliers.

Health Care Financing Administration (HCFA): the federal agency responsible for administering the Medicare program; has some jurisdiction over Medicaid as well. HCFA qualifies some HMOs if federal standards are met.

Healthcare provider: anyone providing medical services, including doctors, nurses, physician's assistants, pharmacists, and therapists.

Health and Human Services (HHS): an umbrella agency of the federal government that is composed of many subagencies (HCFA, Public Health, Office of Education, etc.).

Health Maintenance Organization (HMO): an organized system of healthcare delivery which provides comprehensive health services to voluntarily enrolled members. Each member pays a periodic per capita amount which does not fluctuate in relation to the number or extent of services rendered. There are several types of HMOs, but all share some characteristics. The most significant characteristic relates to the fact that HMOs combine both the delivery and the financing of care in one system; that is, medical services and insurance coverage are furnished by the same organization. Unlike insurance plans, claims are not submitted for reimbursement. Rather, the HMO subscriber pays a fixed monthly amount in advance regardless of the number or type of medical services he or she receives.

Home health agency: a public or private organization that specializes in providing skilled nursing services and therapeutic services such as physical therapy in an individual's home.

Hospice: a program operated by a public agency or private organization that engages primarily in providing pain relief, symptom management, and supportive services for terminally ill individuals and their families.

Indemnity plan: the traditional form of health insurance. In return for a fixed monthly premium, an insurance company pays all or part of each covered employee's healthcare costs.

Independent Practice Associations (IPAs): organizations that are called "open-panel" because a physician's practice is not limited to IPA patients. The physician cares for prepaid enrollees along with fee-for-service patients. There are many variations, but in its most basic form an IPA is a physicians' organization which provides services to HMO enrollees. The HMO pays the IPA a capitation amount; the IPA in turn pays its member physicians, usually on a fee-for-service basis. The physician shares the responsibility for the total cost of care by agreeing to have some portion of each fee withheld and put into a common risk pool, to be redistributed among all the participating physicians if the IPA has a financially successful year. IPA physicians work in their own offices, where they serve both HMO members and fee-for-service patients.

International Classification of Diseases [9th revision, Clinical Modification, 4th edition (ICD-4-CM)]: the diagnosis coding system used by all physicians, hospitals, and related medical facilities.

Limited practitioners: providers licensed to practice within a range of services according to their specific scope of training in areas such as dentistry, chiropractic, podiatry, psychology, social work, and physical therapy.

Managed care: an umbrella term describing reimbursement alternatives to straight fee-for-service; providers participate by contract and are paid on an agreed on flat rate called capitation regardless of the number of patients or frequency of visits. Some plans offer physician reimbursement in a reduced fee-for-service arrangement instead. Managed care also controls the private practice of medicine more than does traditional fee-for-service through gatekeepers, preauthorization, utilization review, and the like.

Mandatory outpatient surgery: a list of surgical procedures that can and should be performed on an outpatient basis established to reduce unnecessary hospital admissions.

Medigap policy: private health insurance designed to supplement Medicare by paying for some of the gaps in medical services not covered by Medicare and some of the patient's copays.

Modified fee-for-service compensation: a system in which physicians are paid on a unit-of-service basis.

Monitoring and peer review committee: a committee made up of licensed physicians experienced in one medical field, formed to serve as an advisor to insurance carriers on quality assurance, medical necessity, and reimbursement issues.

Network model HMO: a system in which existing multispecialty or single specialty group practices have contracts with an HMO to provide certain services at a fixed capitation fee per enrollee. Each group determines its own plan for distributing the income to the individual physicians. Physicians practice in a group facility and see some prepaid patients along with fee-for-service patients.

Operative report: the surgical report and prognosis usually dictated and signed by the attending physician.

Out-of-plan referral authorization: a system in which referrals to specialists who are not participating physicians must be preauthorized by the system medical director.

Outpatient treatment: treatment rendered in a hospital, clinic, or office setting where the patient is admitted, treated, and released on the same day.

Overall (global) physician capitation: a system in which each primary care physician is credited with a monthly capitated amount for each enrollee who selects that physician as his or her primary care physician. The amount is intended to cover the cost of all physician services and is determined actuarially as in the case of primary care capitation. A portion of the capitation is paid to the physician at the beginning of each month, and the remainder is held by the system in a reserve fund to pay for specialist services received by the enrollees of the physician. Any amounts remaining in the fund at the end of the year are paid to the primary care physician, and any deficit is either carried forward into the following year and charged against capitation payments or paid by the physician to the system. This compensation arrangement makes the primary care physician responsible for both the referral and the payment for the referral. As with other compensation methods, overall physician capitation usually includes risksharing between the primary care physician and the system for hospital fund services.

Peer Review Organization (PRO): a group of practicing doctors and other healthcare professionals under contract with the federal government to review the care provided to managed care patients.

Penetration rate: the percentage rate at which eligible employees in an employer group select a system to provide their health coverage.

Physician Hospital Organization (PHO): to achieve the linkage between primary care physicians (PCPs) and hospitals, PHOs are formed to enable hospitals to utilize the PCP gatekeeper approach as they attempt to secure contracts. The PHO allows providers to regain or retain control often relinquished to another type of MCO. The PCPs provide a utilization review function, case management, and quality assurance and serve as a gatekeeper, while the hospital provides the facility, the necessary capital, information gathering, and organizational expertise. Although direct contracting with industry is possible with this structure, it also is possible for a PHO to contract with HMOs or PPOs.

Physician Administrative Organization (PAO): an organization in which, as with an IPA, doctors have an equity interest. A PAO has its own independent management or holding company that conducts business for the physician shareholders or partners. This arrangement allows the doctor to negotiate forcefully for the type and amount of reimbursement, formulate and administer quality and utilization guidelines, perform credentialing and peer review, and even own a hospital. It sometimes acts to procure supplies for the practice or negotiate for malpractice rates. Most prevalent in the western states, PAOs are predicted to be prominent in most metropolitan areas in the next eight to ten years. Doctors often speak highly of these plans because they allow for more autonomy than do other MCOs.

Point-Of-Service (POS) plan: a hybrid between a traditional HMO and a PPO. In a POS plan, the insured is encouraged to seek medical care in a preferred provider network with a gatekeeper, but care may be obtained outside the network at reduced coverage levels and at a higher cost. Often the copay for seeking care outside of the network is 30 percent. A POS plan resembles a PPO but is in actuality an open-ended HMO.

Preadmission review and authorization: in this system, all elective admissions must be reviewed and authorized by the medical director and the enrollee's primary care physician.

Preexisting condition: a condition for which medical advice was given or treatment was recommended by or received from a physician before the effective date of an insurance policy.

Preferred Provider Organization (PPO): in general, a group of healthcare providers (professional or institutional) who agree to provide services to a specific pool of patients (usually employment-based groups) at an agreed-on fee-for-service discounted rate. The patient retains free choice of providers but is given an economic incentive (often first dollar coverage) to utilize member providers. The system has built-in incentives for the provider (a pool of patients, fee-for-service, rapid claims turnaround) and the payer (negotiated discounts). Unlike HMOs, PPOs usually do not involve prepayment.

Primary payor: the insurer or healthcare plan first responsible for making a coverage determination on claims for items and/or services provided to a specific beneficiary (see also *coordination of benefits*).

Primary care capitation: a system in which each primary care physician receives a specified amount each month for each system enrollee who selects that physician as his or her primary care physician. The capitation amount is based on an actuarial determination of the utilization of primary care services for which the primary care physician is responsible and the average cost of those services. A portion of this payment may be withheld and placed in a reserve fund. Specialist physicians continue to receive some form of fee-for-service compensation directly from the managed care system under this system. Usually, their compensation is based on the modified fee-for-service approach. There are usually risk-sharing arrangements between the system and the primary care physicians that allow the physicians to have a share in the specialty care fund and the hospital services fund. The primary care capitation approach provides some opportunities to alter the disparity between cognitive and procedural compensation by allowing capitation payments to be based on a projected increased workload for primary care physicians. These physicians, as case managers, assume a more important role in the medical delivery system, and the capitation rate may be set to reflect this importance.

Primary care case management: a process by which a primary care physician is designated as the enrollee's primary physician and is responsible for providing, managing, and arranging for all the healthcare needs of the enrollee. All referrals to specialists and hospital admissions must be preauthorized by the enrollee's primary care physician. Often referred to as the gatekeeper system.

Prior authorization number: an authorization number which may be required by carriers for major scheduled services. It is required by some insurance carriers before major surgeries. The goal is to give the insurance company time to evaluate whether the surgery is necessary.

Profile year: the twelve-month period which traditional indemnity insurance carriers typically maintain to determine allowable charges.

Reinsurance: acquired by most systems from external insurers to cover all or a portion of claims that exceed certain limits.

Relative Value Scale (RVS): an insurance reimbursement mechanism based on a relative value assigned to each coded service and then multiplied by a conversion factor to determine a fee or an approved amount.

Resource-Based Relative Value Scale (RBRVS): the Medicare-specific RVS data base for determining physicians' payments.

Retrospective reviews: periodic reviews of specific services, tests, or procedures conducted to identify trends and determine whether healthcare resources are being used appropriately.

Self-insured employer: an employer offering medical insurance who may elect to pay medical claims directly instead of contracting with an insurance carrier for health coverage for its employees.

Signature on file: to alleviate the need for signing every claim form, a patient signature made to a statement authorizing the release of medical records and/or the assignment of benefits. The signature is usually retained in registration data in an office or hospital medical record.

Skilled Nursing Facility (SNF): a specially qualified facility which has the staff and equipment to provide skilled nursing care or rehabilitation services and other related health services.

Social HMO: a new concept intended only for the elderly. A social HMO provides comprehensive health and long-term care benefits to Medicare beneficiaries. Unlike other HMOs that enroll Medicare patients, care in a social HMO is reimbursed at 100 percent. Currently four demonstration projects are being funded by the federal government. They are being evaluated for the feasibility of extending them to a broader segment of the Medicare population.

Specialist referral authorization: with this authorization, all referrals of system enrollees to participating specialists, including those made by phone, must be authorized in writing by the enrollee's primary care physician.

Staff model HMO: an HMO in which physicians are direct, salaried employees of the HMO. Physicians deliver care in health centers owned or operated by the HMO and share equipment, medical records, and personnel. Staff and group model HMOs are often referred to as closedpanel HMOs because subscribers are locked into the utilization of the HMO physicians.

Stop-loss: a provision that limits financial exposure to a defined maximum amount above which additional obligations are shared with or assumed by a third party. Reinsurance is an example of stop-loss protection acquired by managed care systems.

Supplemental health insurance: Also called "Medigap" insurance. This is private health insurance designed to fill some of the "gaps" in Medicare coverage. Some Medicare enrollees belong to an HMO to supplement their health insurance.

System reimbursement: a system in which a portion of each payment (usually 10 to 25 percent) is withheld in a reserve fund until the end of the year to protect against overutilization of health services. A physician may receive all, some, or none of the withheld amounts after the end of the year. Utilization experience is generally measured for the overall system but is increasingly measured at both the individual physician level and for the system as a whole in determining the disposition of the withheld reserve. A second modification is that the physician submits his or her bills directly to the system and agrees to accept the system's payment as full payment (except for applicable copayments). Most states require physician contracts to contain a provision that the physician will "look solely to the system for payment" to protect enrollees from financial responsibility. As a result of this provision, physicians can bill system enrollees only for copayments or deductibles regardless of the payment they receive from the system. A third modification is that the compensation agreement usually provides for risk sharing between contracting physicians and the system. With these risk sharing provisions, physicians may receive additional payments if hospital utilization is lower than projected but may lose a portion of the withhold fee if utilization is higher than projected.

System utilization review:

- Concurrent review: all hospital stays are subject to concurrent review throughout the patient's period of confinement based on predetermined criteria to justify hospitalization.
- Ambulatory care review: all outpatient services are reviewed retrospectively to ensure the appropriate utilization of health services.
- Emergency care review: all emergency care services are reviewed concurrently and/or retrospectively to ensure that the services rendered are medically necessary and are performed in the most appropriate setting.

Usual, Customary, and Reasonable (UCR): generic references to an insurance payment mechanism; the lowest of the designated charges determines the approved amount. The usual fee is the physician's submitted charge, the customary is based on the physician's history of charges for the given services, and the reasonable refers to area fees for the service.

Utilization management procedures: a system in which most managed care systems establish procedures for reviewing the medical care of enrollees to ensure that care is given in the most appropriate setting by the most appropriate provider.

Utilization Review Organization (URO): the process by which decisions on hospital admission are examined in advance by an external reviewer. This review is accountable to an employer, insurer, HMO, PPO, IPA, or other entity responsible for all or most of the cost of care.

Waiting period: a specified period in which preexisting and/or new conditions are not covered by an insurance plan.

APPENDIX C

HMOs and Dispute Resolution Provisions

Medical Malpractice Arbitration and HMOs

Most of the states have enacted legislation to facilitate the resolution of medical malpractice disputes. These laws establish minimum and maximum limits for claims, arbitration procedures for the resolution of disputes between patients and physicians, pretrial screening panels, and other mechanisms intended to discourage meritless claims, speed up prosecution of the initial claim to a final judgment, and reduce the costs involved in malpractice suits.

Despite findings of unconstitutionality by the courts in some jurisdictions, most states have successfully implemented these laws. Adverse judicial decisions have often stemmed from findings that required arbitration or the right to trial by jury.

The broad terms and general language of some medical malpractice arbitration provisions leave them open to judicial interpretation. This is particularly true in regard to the determination of whether these laws affect HMOs as entities providing healthcare services or apply only to the individual physician or other medical professional who contracts with an HMO. In addition, even if malpractice arbitration provisions clearly apply to HMOs, they may conflict with a state HMO Act's mandated internal grievance procedures or arbitration provisions.

A complete analysis of the impact of malpractice arbitration laws on HMOs requires consideration of issues beyond applicability. The nature of the arbitration requirement is crucial (whether arbitration is compulsory, whether the decision of an arbitration panel is binding on the parties involved, and the effect of the rulings of a pretrial screening panel on subsequent litigation).

To comprehend the nature of the issues involved, it is necessary to define and explain some of the terms that appear in medical malpractice arbitration laws.

Arbitration: Most jurisdictions have general arbitration statutes that allow parties to submit controversies to an unbiased panel or group which will make a final determination of the claim. Several states have also created specialized medical malpractice arbitration panels, which are usually composed of health professionals and lawyers. The parties submit medical malpractice claims to these panels on either a voluntary or a compulsory basis, depending on the requirements of the law. The panel may make a binding decision which is subject to review by a trial court.

Most states with voluntary malpractice arbitration provisions have clauses that stipulate the length of the period during which a party may rescind an arbitration agreement. Submission to arbitration of present and/or future claims is voluntary in such cases. If a party does not opt out by rescinding the agreement within the specified period, compliance with the arbitration procedures becomes mandatory. This differs from the situation in states that mandate arbitration of medical malpractice claims in which a pre-existing agreement is nonexistent.

Pretrial screening panels: Submission of claims to a pretrial screening panel in jurisdictions where statutes authorize such panels is usually a prerequisite to filing a malpractice claim but is generally not a substitute for binding arbitration or judicial action. These panels give the plaintiff some idea of the likelihood of winning on the merits and attempt to reach an agreement between the parties before the trial. The panel's findings are often used as evidence at a later trial. Although the determination of a pretrial screening panel is not binding, some states permit a transfer of the matter from a pretrial screening panel to an arbitration panel whose decision is binding.

HMOs, grievance procedures, and arbitration: Most state HMO laws require the establishment of an internal grievance procedure. This usually takes the form of a complaint system for the resolution of written grievances initiated by enrollees concerning healthcare services. This limited system is distinct from an arbitration or pretrial screening panel. Some HMO acts require an arbitration procedure, but most require only a grievance procedure. When the HMO law does not expressly apply the provisions of these other arbitration laws to HMOs, statutory interpretation becomes crucial.

In some states the HMO law or malpractice arbitration law clearly subjects HMOs to arbitration and pretrial screening procedures. Other states do not mention HMOs specifically but apply the law to "licensed health facilities" or all "healthcare providers" and "healthcare institutions." In these cases it may be easier to determine whether the law applies to HMOs. Several other states, however, have adopted legislation that necessitates more careful analysis. For example, several state arbitration laws apply to disputes involving "hospitals" but may leave that term undefined or define it differently in other state laws. A judicial or administrative opinion may be necessary to resolve the issue of applicability of the law to HMOs in those states.

Still other states apply the arbitration law only to physicians, nurses, and other individual practitioners. While the HMO as an entity may be exempt from the law, the applicability of arbitration provisions to the contracting or staff physicians can affect any HMO.

Dispute Resolution Provisions

Charts I and II illustrate current statutory provisions concerning HMOs and the mechanisms for resolving disputes through grievance procedures, medical malpractice arbitration laws, and pretrial screening panels. Chart I lists states with HMO acts or enabling laws that require internal grievance or complaint resolution procedures and/or arbitration provisions,

KEY: ○ Yes ● No

Chart I: Arbitration Provisions in State Enabling Laws[1]

STATE	HMO Act	Internal Grievance Procedure in Enabling Law	Arbitration Provision in Enabling Law
ALABAMA	○	○	●
ALASKA	○	○	●
ARIZONA	○	●	●
ARKANSAS	○	○	●
CALIFORNIA	○	○	○
COLORADO	○	○	●
CONNECTICUT	○	○	○
DELAWARE	○	●[2]	●
DISTRICT OF COLUMBIA	●	●	●
FLORIDA	○	○	○
GEORGIA	○	○	●
HAWAII	●	●	●
IDAHO	○	○	●
ILLINOIS	○	○	●
INDIANA	●	○[3]	●

Chart I: *(Continued)*

STATE	HMO Act	Internal Grievance Procedure in Enabling Law	Arbitration Provision in Enabling Law
IOWA	○	○	●
KANSAS	○	○	●
KENTUCKY	○	●[2]	●
LOUISIANA	○	○	●
MAINE	○	○	●
MARYLAND	○	○	●
MASSACHUSETTS	○	●[2]	●
MICHIGAN	○	○	●
MINNESOTA	○	○	○
MISSISSIPPI	○	●[2]	●
MISSOURI	○	○	●
MONTANA	○	○	●
NEBRASKA	○	○	●
NEVADA	○	○	○
NEW HAMPSHIRE	○	○	●
NEW JERSEY	○	○	●
NEW MEXICO	○	○	●
NEW YORK	○	○	○
NORTH CAROLINA	○	○	●
NORTH DAKOTA	○	○	●
OHIO	○	○	●
OKLAHOMA	○	●[2]	●[2]
OREGON	●	●	●
PENNSYLVANIA	○	○	●[2]
RHODE ISLAND	○	○	●
SOUTH CAROLINA	○	○	●
SOUTH DAKOTA	○	○	○
TENNESSEE	○	○	●
TEXAS	○	○	●
UTAH	○	○	●
VERMONT	○	○	●
VIRGINIA	○	○	●[2]
WASHINGTON	○	○	○
WEST VIRGINIA	○	○	●[2]
WISCONSIN	●	●[4]	●
WYOMING	○	○	●
PUERTO RICO	○	○	●

[1]Enabling law means the HMO law or other law under which HMOs may form.
[2]Agency regulations contain internal grievance procedure/arbitration provision.
[3]Implied.
[4]Found at Section 609.15—not an enabling act.

with a column to remind the user of those states which have HMO Acts. Chart II examines two possible statutory mechanisms for the resolution of claims against healthcare providers: medical malpractice arbitration provisions and pretrial screening panels.

Chart II does not include general arbitration statutes. Most states have general arbitration laws that are designed to resolve myriad disputes. Only the statutes that provide specifically for application to medical malpractice claims appear here. Chart II indicates the existence of such laws and their statutory citations, whether arbitration is binding and/or compulsory, and whether the laws apply to HMOs. Individual citations are given for malpractice arbitration provisions located in code sections separate from pretrial screening laws.

Compulsory arbitration and pretrial screening means that all malpractice claims must go through these processes. The third column identifies states that have this type of statutory scheme. Normally an enforceable court judgment can be obtained when an arbitration panel that has power to bind the parties renders judgment. The fourth column details provisions authorizing binding arbitration.

The fifth column lists states that specifically apply an arbitration or screening panel provision to HMOs. In cases where a state statute is less specific concerning the persons and entities covered by the law, a footnote indicates that a "provider" may be considered a partnership, corporation, association, facility, institution, or other entity authorized by law to provide professional services. An asterisk indicates that the language of the statute is open to interpretation regarding the inclusion of HMOs. In Chart II, a blank block indicates that research to date has not identified a relevant provision.

Chart II: Non-HMO Act Medical Malpractice Arbitration/Screening Panel Provisions

Key: ○ Yes ● No
▲ Unclear/Justiciable Issue

State	Medical Malpractice Arbitration Provisions	Medical Malpractice Pre-Trial Screening Panel Provisions	Arbitration/ Screening Submission Compulsory	Arbitrators' Decision Binding	Arbitration/ Screening Panel Applies to HMOs
ALABAMA—Ala. Code §§6-5-480 et seq.	○		●[1]	○	○[2]
ALASKA—Alaska Stat. §§09.55.530 et seq.	○	○[3]	○	○	○
ARIZONA—[REPEALED]					
ARKSANSAS					
CALIFORNIA—Cal. Civ. Proc. §1295	○		○	○	○

Chart II: ***(Continued)***

Key: ○ Yes ● No
▲ Unclear/Justiciable Issue

State	Medical Malpractice Arbitration Provisions	Medical Malpractice Pre-Trial Screening Panel Provisions	Arbitration/ Screening Submission Compulsory	Arbitrators' Decision Binding	Arbitration/ Screening Panel Applies to HMOs
COLORADO—Colo. Rev. Stat. §13-64-403	○		○	○	○[4]
CONNECTICUT—Conn. Gen. Stat. §§38-19a et seq.		○[5]			○[6]
DELAWARE—Del. Code Ann. tit. 18, §§6801 et seq.		○[7]	y[7]		○[8]
DISTRICT OF COLUMBIA					
FLORIDA—Fla. Stat. Ann. §§766.106 et seq.	○	○[9]	○[10]		▲[11]
GEORGIA—Ga. Code Ann. §§401 et seq.	○[12]		●	○	▲[13]
HAWAII—Haw. Rev. Stat. §§671-1 et seq.	○	○[14]	○		○
IDAHO—Idaho Gen. Laws Ann. §§6-1001 et seq.		○	○		▲[15]
ILLINOIS—Ill. Ann. Stat. §§10-201 et seq.	○			○[16]	○[17]
INDIANA—Ind. Code Ann. §§16-9.5-9-1 et seq.		○[18]	○[19]		▲[20]
IOWA					
KANSAS—Kan. Stat. Ann. §§65-4901 et seq.		○[21]			○
KENTUCKY					
LOUISIANA—La. Rev. Stat. Ann. §§9.4230 et seq.	○			○	▲[22]
La. Rev. Stat. Ann. §40.1299.47		○[23]	○[24]		○
MAINE—Me. Rev. Stat. tit. 24, §§2851 et seq.		○[25]			▲[26]
MARYLAND—Md. Cts. Jud. Proc. Code Ann. §§3-2A-01 et seq.	○		○	○	▲[27]
MASSACHUSETTS—Mass. Gen. Laws Ann. Ch. 231, §608		○[28]	○		○[29]
MICHIGAN—Mich. Comp. Laws §§600.5040 et seq.	○			○	○[30]
MINNESOTA					
MISSISSIPPI					
MISSOURI					
MONTANA—Mont. Rev. Code Ann. §§27-6-101		○[31]	○		○[32]
NEBRASKA—Neb. Rev. Stat. §§44-2840 et seq.		○[33]	○		○[34]

Chart II: ***(Continued)***

Key: ○ Yes ● No
▲ Unclear/Justiciable Issue

State	Medical Malpractice Arbitration Provisions	Medical Malpractice Pre-Trial Screening Panel Provisions	Arbitration/ Screening Submission Compulsory	Arbitrators' Decision Binding	Arbitration/ Screening Panel Applies to HMOs
NEVADA—Nev. Rev. Stat. Ann. §§41A.003 et seq.		○[35]	○		○[36]
NEW HAMPSHIRE—N.H. Rev. Stat. Ann. §§519-A: 1 et seq.		○[37]			▲[38]
NEW JERSEY					
NEW MEXICO—N.M. Stat. Ann. §§41-5-1 et seq.		○[39]			○[40]
NEW YORK—N.Y. Civ. Prac. L&R §§7551 et seq.	○		○	○	○
N.Y. Jud. Law §148-a		○[41]	○		▲[42]
NORTH CAROLINA					
NORTH DAKOTA					
OHIO—Ohio Rev. Code Ann. §§2711.21 et seq.	○		●[43]	●	○
OKLAHOMA					
OREGON					
PENNSYLVANIA—Pa. Stat. Ann. tit. 40, §§1301.308 et seq.[44]	○		○	○	○
RHODE ISLAND					
SOUTH CAROLINA					
SOUTH DAKOTA—S.D. Compiled Laws Ann. §§21-25B-1 et seq.	○[45]			○	○
TENNESSEE					
TEXAS					
UTAH—Utah Code Ann. §§78-14-1 et seq.		○[46]	○	●	○[47]
VERMONT—Vt. Stat. Ann. tit. 12, §§7001 et seq.	○			○	○
VIRGINIA—Va. Code §§8.01-81.1 et seq.		○[48]			○
WASHINGTON					
WEST VIRGINIA					
WISCONSIN—Wisc. Stat. Ann. §§655.42 et seq.		○	○		○
WYOMING—Wyo. Stat. §§9-2-1501 et seq.[49]		○[50]	○		○
PUERTO RICO—P.R. Laws Ann. tit. 26 §§4110 et seq.	○			○	▲[51]

[1]After a claim is made, parties may enter into binding arbitration.

[2]Applies to hospitals, which by definition includes HMOs.
[3]HMO enrollees may execute a hospital arbitration agreement (revocable by enrollee within 30 days of execution) before admission of receiving services. The court, in lieu of an arbitration agreement, must appoint an expert advisory panel.
[4]"Health care provider" means any person licensed or certified by the State of Colorado to deliver health care and any clinic, health dispensary, or health facility licensed by the State. The term includes any professional corporation or other professional entity comprised of such health care providers.
[5]The panel's conclusion is admissible in evidence if it is unanimous.
[6]"Health care provider" includes any person, corporation, facility, or institution licensed by the State to provide health care or professional services. The statute specifically includes IPAs.
[7]Submission to panel compulsory upon motion of either party.
[8]"Health care provider" means persons or corporations licensed by the State to provide health care.
[9]Defendant's insurer/self-insured must have a presuit screening procedure.
[10]Upon either party's motion, the court may order nonbinding arbitration.
[11]"Medical malpractice claim" is one arising out of the rendering or failure to render medical care or services.
[12]The parties may agree to arbitration. Such agreement may be made only after the dispute arises.
[13]"Medical malpractice claim" is one arising from health, medical, dental, or surgical service, diagnosis, prescription, treatment, or care.
[14]The panel's conclusion is inadmissible at trial.
[15]Applies to claims against physicians and surgeons practicing in Idaho or licensed acute care general hospitals operating in Idaho.
[16]Every arbitration agreement must require that all parties abide by the decision of the arbitration panel.
[17]"Health care provider" means a person, partnership, corporation, or other entity lawfully engaged in the practice of medicine, surgery, etc.
[18]A report of the expert opinion reached by the panel is admissible in court.
[19]A claimant may commence a malpractice action without presentation to the review panel if all parties to agree, or if damages claimed are less than $15,000.
[20]Applies to all malpractice claims against "health care providers".
[21]The screening panel's written report is admissible in court and panel members are subject to subpoena.
[22]Applies to controversies involving medical contracts and dental contracts.
[23]The screening panel's conclusion is admissible at trial.
[24]Pretrial panel is compulsory, unless the dispute is submitted to arbitration.
[25]The panel's findings are admissible in court if unanimous.
[26]Applies to claims against health care practitioners and health care providers, their employees and agents.
[27]HMO is not within definition of health care provider per case law.
[28]The panel determines if the evidence raises a legitimate question of liability. The panel's decision is admissible at trial.
[29]"Provider of health care" includes a person, facility, or institution licensed to provide health care.
[30]"Health care provider" means a person, partnership, or corporation lawfully engaged in the practice of medicine, surgery, etc.
[31]The panel's decision is not admissible in court.
[32]"Health care provider" means a physician or a health care facility.
[33]The panel's decision is admissible as evidence at trial.
[34]"Health care provider" means a corporation or entity authorized to provide professional medical services by physicians.
[35]This statute was scheduled to expire June 30, 1989. A finding for the plaintiff requires a settlement conference if a court action is filed. The panel's findings are admissible in court.
[36]Health care provider means a person, corporation, organization, facility, or institution licensed or certified to provide health care or professional services.
[37]Transcripts of proceedings may be used in subsequent litigation.
[38]Applies to professional malpractice claims (lawyer, doctor, dentist).
[39]The panel's findings are not admissible at trial.
[40]"Health care provider" means a person, organization, facility, or institution licensed to provide health care.
[41]The panel's recommendation is admissible at trial.
[42]Applies to medical malpractice actions.
[43]This section applies to any medical, dental, optometric, or chiropractic claim if all parties agree. The arbitration board's decision is not admissible at trial.
[44]Parts of this statute have been held to be unconstitutional.
[45]ADO option 76-96 stated that HMO enrollee contracts cannot make arbitration agreements a prerequisite to treatment.
[46]The panel's findings are not admissible at trial and are not subject to judicial or other review.
[47]"Health care provider" includes any person, partnership, association, corporation, or other facility or institution that renders health care or professional services.
[48]Screening decisions are admissible at trial.
[49]A 1988 court decision held that this statute violated the equal protection clause of the Wyoming Constitution.
[50]The panel's decision is not admissible in court.
[51]Applies to claims for fault of negligence due to professional medicohospital malpractice.

Selected Arbitration Cases

Arizona	*Eastin v. Bloomfield,* 520 P.2d 744 (1977)
California	*Herbert v. Superior Court (Kaiser Found.),* 215 Cal. Rptr. 477 (Cal. Ct. App. 1985)
	Harris v. Superior Court (Mirsaidi), 233 Cal. Rptr. 186 (Cal. Ct. App. 1986) [Maxicare]
Florida	*Aldana v. Holub,* 381 So.2d 231 (1980)
Illinois	*Wright v. Central Du Page Hosp. Assn.,* 63 Ill. 2d 313, 347 N.E.2d 736 (1976)
Indiana	*Johnson v. St. Vincent Hosp.,* 404 N.E.2d 1024 (Ind. Ct. App. 1981)
Louisiana	*Everett v. Goldman,* 359 So.2d 1256 (1978)
Maryland	*Group Health Assn. v. Blumenthal,* 295 Md 104, 453 A.2d 1198 (1938)
Michigan	*Morris v. Metriyakool,* 418 Mich. 423, 344 N.W.2d 736 (1984)
	Morgan v. Kamil, 375 N.W.2d 378 (Mich. Ct. App. 1985)
Missouri	*Cardinal Glennon Mem. Hosp. for Children v. Gaertner,* 583 S.W.2d 107 (1979)
Montana	*Linder v. Smith,* 38 St. Rep 912 (1982)
New York	*Gronne v. Adams,* 793 F.2d 74 (C.A.2, N.Y. 1986)
	Cochrane v. Gothan, 502 N.Y.S.2d 849 (N.Y. App. Div. 1986)
	Amato v. Chafel, 502 N.Y.S.2d 851 (N.Y.App. Div. 1986)
Ohio	*Beatty v. Akron City Hospital,* 424 N.E.2d 586 (1981)
Pennsylvania	*Mattos v. Thompson,* 421 A.2d 190 (Pa. 1980)
	Heller v. Frankston, 475 A.2d 1291 (Pa. 1984)
Rhode Island	*Boucher v. Sayeed,* 459 A.2d 87 (R.I. 1983)
Wisconsin	*State ex rel. Strykowski v. Wilkie,* 261 N.W.2d 434 (1978)

APPENDIX D

Sources for Managed Care Information

The primary regulator of HMOs in a state is not the only agency which can offer assistance or information to medical practices. To obtain further information regarding managed care plans operating in a particular area, a practice can contact one or more of the following agencies.

Office of Prepaid Health Care Operations and Oversight
Health Care Financing Administration
Room 4406 Cohen Building
330 Independent Avenue, S.W.
Washington, D.C. 20201
(202) 619–0845

The Medical Management Institute
1125 Cambridge Square
Alpharetta, Georgia 30201
(404) 475–1220

The Medical Management Institute publishes a monthly newletter with updates and effects managed care development have on the private practice of medicine; at a subscription rate of $125 per year.

HCFA maintains a cumulative listing of federally qualified health maintenance organizations that is updated twice a year in April and September. It is available free of charge.

American Managed Care and Review Association (AMCRA)
1227 25th Street, N.W.
Suite 610
Washington, D.C. 20037–1156
(202) 728–0506
(202) 728–0609 (fax)

AMCRA publishes a directory of several types of organizations involved with managed care including HMOs, IPAs, PPOs, and Utilization Review Organizations. The 1992 edition was priced at $195.

Department of Health Care Delivery
Division of Health Policy and Program Evaluation
American Medical Association
535 North Dearborn Street
Chicago, IL 60610
(312) 645–4718

The AMA publishes a book entitled Physician's Resource Guide to Health Delivery Systems which may offer further information and has available a variety of practice development and educational videos for its members.

Group Health Association of America
1129 20th Street, N.W., Suite 600
Washington, D.C. 20036
(202) 778–3247

GHAA publishes HMO Managers Letter, a bimonthly newsletter for managed care organizations, at a subscription price of $125 per year.

Index